MY LIFE COACH

WEARS A TUTU

A Book for Coaches: Be Yourself, Make Money & Have Fun
Jesse Gros, M.A.

Copyright © 2016 by Jesse Gros.

All rights reserved. No part of this book may be reproduced, distributed, or transmitted in any form or by any means, including photocopying, recording, or other electronic or mechanical methods, without the prior written permission of the publisher or copyright holders, except in the case of brief quotations embodied in critical reviews and certain other noncommercial uses permitted by copyright law. For permission requests, write to the publisher, addressed "Attention: Permissions Coordinator," at the address below.

 **Jesse**Gros

www.jessegros.com
Los Angeles, California

Cover Design: Alexandria Zech
Book Designer and Illustrations: Matt Hinrichs

My Life Coach Wears a Tutu / Jesse Gros. – 1st ed.
ISBN 978-0-9897093-1-6

FOR DEVON

Introduction

This Is the Book I Wish I Had Five Years Ago

When I left my work in the insurance industry, I knew next to nothing about how to thrive as a coach — not just financially, but spiritually, emotionally and creatively. I was a very slow starter. So slow, that I almost quit after my second year. I think I had five clients during my first 24 months. I was so sure that this was the profession for me, and yet it seemed like I really wasn't any good at it.

Since then, a lot has changed.

I have led retreats all over the world, worked with professional athletes, CEOs and social change-makers. I wrote an award-winning book and I welcomed my first child into the world.

This book is about what I learned in the space between.

Each chapter is packed full of bite-sized chunks of inspiration, powerful distinctions and useful tools for you. Take your time, chew slowly and repeat. Some of these chapters I still read over and over as a reminder when I get off course — which happens a lot with a toddler running around the house!

Before We Begin

So… What's With The Tutu?

My tutu fascination started at the Burning Man Festival on the famous "Tutu Tuesday," (www.burningman.com) where tens of thousands of people of all backgrounds, professions, and lifestyles celebrate the day sporting their best tutu! There is a freedom and a playfulness that shows up in people when they are wearing these fabulous little ballerina ball gowns.

And, it doesn't matter if you are a billionaire tech giant, a schoolteacher, a famous author going undercover or a politician from Maine (all people I met in full tutu regalia). When people are sporting tutus, the barriers drop and they can just be themselves.

So that's what we are going to do in this book. We are going to drop the pretense, let you exhale and connect with the joy of being a coach!

Woo-Woo — Woo-woo is a term I use a lot in this book. When I say woo-woo, I'm talking about spiritual practices that supersede our rational mind and bring us to elevated states of consciousness. These are things like meditation, mantras, certain forms of prayer, breathwork and accessing your intuition — to name a few. For many years, I was skeptical about the practical value of these practices and wrote them off as soft tools for the ungrounded. Wow! Was I wrong.

"Highly effective woo-woo" are practices I use with individual and corporate clients, that I have found with over a decade of personal experimentation and use, give you the most bang for your buck. These tools are powerful, effective and are likely to be off of most people's radar.

Moolah — Imagine getting well paid to be the most fully-expressed version of yourself. That's what I am doing in my life and that's the work I am doing with my clients. It has taken me a while to shake off the inner voice that says I can't get paid to be me. I had this long-standing fear that, in order to be successful I somehow had to sell out or be some version of me that was "acceptable" in the world. I find that the opposite is true. The more I am myself and just plain reject any part of my business that doesn't light me up, the more successful I become.

*All of the stories in this book are true, as I remember them. However, many of the names and personal details have been changed to ensure confidentiality.

Introducing... DR. LOGAN

The little guy on the front cover is Dr. Logan. He's going to be our guide for the next ten chapters.

So... who is this Dr. Logan character?

In 2005, out on a massive dry lakebed known as "the Playa," in the middle of the Black Rock Desert, I showed up with my tent, food for a week, a box of costumes and a gift to share. That year the Burning Man Festival theme was "Psyche: The Conscious, Subconscious & Unconscious," so I created a portable coaching office on wheels, complete with chairs, a table and a cooler for beverages. My first coaching gig!

Wanting to legitimize my mobile coaching practice, I wrote, "Just Ask Dr. Logan" on the back of my cart. I used my middle name because Dr. Gros just sounded, well... gross. After coaching a young couple who were experiencing cold feet about their upcoming nuptials, they asked, "Are you a real doctor?" I responded, "Nope. But I play one at Burning Man!" We all had a big laugh and they ran off to the chapel.

That's how *Dr. Logan* was born.

TABLE OF CONTENTS

"Believe nothing, no matter where you read it, or who said it, no matter if I have said it, unless it agrees with your own reason and your own common sense."

– **Buddha**

THE GURU FALLACY

1

One of the BIG LIES about coaching is that you have to be some kind of a guru or an expert in order to coach people. Coaches say things like, "If I had *this* degree," or, "Once I get my life to *that* level, *then* I will feel really confident coaching people." The illusion is that somehow you have to "have it all together" in order to coach others to improve their lives. It's just not true.

I call this misunderstanding the **Guru Fallacy**.

When I share this with coaches, the question I often hear is, "Why would someone hire me or work with me unless I project the confidence of big success or mastery?" I started out coaching with the same question myself and this thought plagued me for years. I drew the false conclusion that in order to succeed, I had to be some version of my first mentor, Tony Robbins — a larger than life, almost superhero-like character, who is one of the most successful motivational speakers and coaches of all time.

Let's just say I set the bar *really* high. And as a result, I spent a lot of energy bouncing back and forth trying to be like him and falling into despair that I wasn't even close. It was exhausting. It wasn't hard for anyone who was paying attention to see what I was up to. "Hey, look at that guy pretending to be somebody he's not. I think I'll hire him to help me do the same!"

Years later, after I had come down from my manic Tony Robbins phase, I enrolled in the life coaching program of Martha Beck, one of Oprah's mentors. After completing her program, I remember thinking, "I want my career to be like hers — more grounded and soulful." The day after the program ended, I had a chilling thought: "She has her PhD from Harvard! I'm never going to have that." My mind created the story, "must-have-PHD-from-Harvard" to be a successful coach. The guru fallacy had struck again. I was paralyzed.

"YOU ONLY HAVE TO BE 2 STEPS AHEAD OF SOMEONE TO HELP THEM."

The Two Steps Rule

I shared these two stories with a mentor of mine. She looked me squarely in the eye and said, "You only have to be two steps ahead of someone to help them. What you are trying to do is go from zero to hero. Slow down." I could feel my whole body go numb for a second as this new realization washed over me, cleansing me of a limiting belief that had plagued me for years.

Recently a client asked me, "How will I know if I am two steps ahead of someone?" You will know because they will naturally be attracted to you and your work. If they are ahead of you, or at the same level as you, then they will know intuitively that you cannot help them and they won't be interested. You don't have to worry about attracting clients outside your ability to help them.

The same client asked, "What if they catch up?" One of two things will happen: they will either push you into your own growth and you will grow faster with them at your heels or they will catch up and maybe even pass you. When that happens, your work with them is done.

The Weird Law of Client Attraction

Don't be surprised when you attract clients who need help with challenges that mirror your own unresolved issues! They may bring it up in your first meeting, or it may pop up as a complete surprise later in your work together. When this happens, consider it a gift that is gently — or not so gently — pushing you into your own growth.

Want to grow fast as a coach? Take on clients who are right at the edge of your own growth curve. These are the clients who will scare you and challenge you every time you meet.

Disciples vs. Clients

If you project the image of "I am the Guru," then you will likely get disciples. You will get people who want to follow and stay followers. The mantra is: "Guru, you tell me what to do, how to be and I will project all that I want for my life onto you, rather than seeing the master that already lives in me." That's not coaching. Coaching is about helping your clients see the "Guru" in *themselves*, and connecting them with their own resourcefulness.

And when they do… that's when you get out of the way.

Don't Fake It Till You Make It

"Fake it till you make it" is one of the predominant success formulas in the coaching world. When I started out I thought I had to "fake it" in order to succeed. I saw successful coaches doing it, so I mimicked them. I always felt like a fraud. Sadly, I misunderstood my discomfort as a weakness, something to be overcome, rather than a symptom of my highly acute radar for personal integrity. Once I stopped making myself wrong, I found another way.

Catherine, a new coach, created a unique personal growth travel adventure business based in India. When I spoke with her, she had been working on this business for over a year and didn't have one single sign-up, despite the dozens of enrollment conversations she had had with potential clients. Her website was designed to give the illusion that her company was a big venture that had been running for years. In her conversations with potential clients she pumped herself up as a successful coach who had already run trips. Even though it made her uncomfortable, she felt like she had to do this to look professional.

I shared with her, "If someone is going to spend thousands of dollars and trust you to care for their physical and mental well-being, there has to be a very high level of trust. Right now, you don't have it."

Catherine stopped posturing, cleaned up her website and changed her focus from impressing to connecting. A year later she called me to share that she had just returned from taking three clients to India on a life-changing retreat!

The Over-Labeler

Have you ever seen someone trying so hard to look successful that it almost hurts to watch? Another iteration of "Fake it till you make it" shows up in the over-labeler. You know one when you see one because they have a virtual billboard of personal labels tagged on after their name, like an advertisement for a trick dog at the circus. "Come see the amazing Coachdini, as she performs a myriad of amazing tricks!"

Learning Happens Both Ways

Coaching is not preaching. It's not teaching. It's parallel learning that happens between the coach and the client.

CEO and coach James Barlow shares: "I think the biggest thing that no one told me about coaching is that learning from your clients is such an incredible opportunity. The fallacy is that as a coach you need to be all-knowing. Being a great coach means that you have to learn about the person and having that unquenchable thirst for understanding someone's personal realities and perspectives. That opportunity to learn from them creates the magical dynamic where they KNOW how much you care about them and have their interests at heart."

What If I'm Star Struck by My Client?

"What if my new client is someone I greatly admire and there is a part of me that can't believe I was hired to coach him?" This is what I call a high quality problem! It has happened to me multiple times.

I was once hired to work with a major Hollywood

director and this is the advice that helped me not pee my pants the whole time: Remember, you are good at what you do and your client is good at what he or she does. If your client is a filmmaker, for example, it does not mean that their skills in cinema help them navigate their own inner landscape. That's your job, that's your area of expertise. Skills and fame don't cross over.

Funny Coaching Moment:

I met the filmmaker I mentioned above at his home for a one-on-one session. After our session, the director and his assistant got up and left the room. I took notes for a minute and when I lifted my head, everyone was gone. The house cleaners, assistants — everyone! It was eerie. I wandered around the house for several minutes until I found an unlocked door. When I stepped outside, the door automatically closed behind me and locked. All of the cars were gone and the massive 10-foot tall gate was closed! Locked in, I popped the cover on the electric gate box, found the fireman's switch and I was free. This director is known to be a trickster, so I wondered the entire time if everyone was up in the control room on the second floor watching me on camera, seeing if I could figure out my escape route!

Guru Fallacy Debunkers #1 — Fit

A well-known psychological study showed that the most important factor in the success of clients working with a coach or therapist is *fit*. Fit is defined as: the degree to which two people are compatible with each other. That's it. The notoriety, education and methodology of the healer were less important than a genuine connection with the client.

Guru Fallacy Debunkers #2 — Be a Lamppost

Still not totally convinced that you don't have to be some kind of guru to really help people? Consider the results of another well-known study: half of the participants had weekly sessions with therapists and the other half had weekly sessions talking about their challenges to a lamppost. At the end of the study, participants were asked to rate their experience and share about how their lives had changed from their participation. It turned out both groups rated their improvement and experience almost exactly the same!

Just listen.

Five Steps to Becoming a World-Class Listener

When I started coaching I was, by my own admission, a lousy listener. I worried that I could never be a good coach. Listening is a skill, not an inborn trait. It can be learned and perfected.

1. Listen between the lines. Focus less on the words the other person is saying and more on the subtle hints and how your body reacts to things they say.

2. Slow your response. If you catch yourself just waiting for your chance to speak, stop, readjust, take a breath and listen.

3. Perception checking. Check in with the other person any time you don't feel crystal clear about what they are saying. "I just want to check in with you… what I hear you saying is…" They will let you know if you heard them correctly. Try this out the next time you get in an argument with your partner. It works wonders.

4. No fixing. Know that the person you are listening to has all the resources to heal themselves. People don't need to be rescued, just guided back to their own resourcefulness.

5. Take the high road. Focus on the highest essence of the person you are listening to. Even when they are showing up as an upset or a confused version of themselves, focus on their loving essence and see if you can hold them in your highest regard.

Show Up and Do Your Thing — EVERY DAY

On the flip side of the Guru Fallacy is a very real phenomenon that grips new coaches as well as professionals.

In his book, *Steal Like an Artist*, author and astute thinker, Austin Kleon, shares, "There's this very real thing that runs rampant in educated people. It's called the **'imposter syndrome.'**" The clinical definition is: "a psychological phenomenon in which people are unable to internalize their accomplishments." It means you feel like a phony, like you are just winging it, that you really don't have any idea what you are doing regardless of your level of education or skill.

Ask anyone doing truly creative work, and they'll tell you the truth. They don't know where the good stuff comes from. *They just show up to do their thing. Every day.*

"Hell, there are no rules here - we're trying to accomplish something."

– Thomas A. Edison

Welcome to the Wild West

In the early 1800s the western United States was a place for people to explore the open frontier, where there were riches to be made, where men were free to live their lives as they chose. This wild landscape attracted gold prospectors, farmers, trappers, snake oil salesmen, bounty hunters, wranglers, robbers, booze-makers and carnival troupes that toured from town to town. It was not a life for the faint of heart, but rather a calling for those who thrived in an open space — men and women with vision that felt stifled by the constraints of organized society. My guess is if you were drawn to pick up this book, there is a part of you that connects with those freedom-loving folk.

However, if you are someone who thrives on structure and lots of rules, then coaching may be a rough ride for you.

Here's why…

There Are No Rules!

Coaching is the Wild West of self-improvement. There is no governing board that monitors the profession, there is no certification needed to be a coach. There are no state boards, no national exam, no licensing, no review board, no enforced code of ethics, zero, zilch, nada.

As you can imagine, with all of this freedom comes the GOOD, the BAD and the UGLY. (I just can't get enough of these cowboy metaphors.) Also included is THE WAY THROUGH — what I have discovered as a clean, honest path through the wide-open spaces and treacherous quicksand of the shadowy side of coaching.

THE GOOD

"Everybody can be great, because anybody can serve. You don't have to have a college degree to serve. You don't have to make your subject and verb agree to serve. You only need a heart full of grace. A soul generated by love."

– Dr. Martin Luther King

If You Say You Are a Coach… YOU ARE

The great news is if you want to be a coach, unlike a therapist, you don't have to commit to years of schooling and thousands of hours of internship work. The barrier to entry is… well… there is no barrier to entry. You don't even need a business card or an office. If you want in, you are in. "Welcome to coaching, coach!"

Alisa, a former CTO of a well-known search engine, left her career to travel the world for a year and a half with her husband. When they returned to the U.S., she had several job offers waiting for her. Not interested in returning to the high-stress life she left behind, she turned them ALL down.

Within weeks, she was offered a consulting/coaching contract with a tech company. She had never seen herself as a "coach," but her new client did, so she figured she would give it a go. She went to the library, checked out ten books on coaching and pulled the best from what she read. That day she updated her LinkedIn profile to include the word "coach." Then, her consulting contract fell through, but her new title was out in the world. Within a week, three people contacted her about coaching. She was shocked! All she had done was add the word "coach" to her online profile. She signed her first three-month client a week later.

Her client shared that he wanted to have her help him climb the corporate ladder, like she had. After listening carefully, she asked him a simple but powerful question, "Why?" This sent him to inquire a bit deeper. Having just left the corporate circle to travel the world, she was familiar with ladder climbing for its own sake. She sent him home with some homework: to look a bit deeper into his own core values and see what he really wanted from the next chapter of his life. Rather than just help him execute his plan, she intuitively asked the deeper question, which may have changed her client's life forever.

If you say you are a coach… you are.

Gut Check

I want to be clear that getting good training and many hours under your belt working with people is crucial. The quality of your work and the results people get while working with you will ultimately stand as the testament to who you are as a coach. There is no substitute for quality. AND... I want you to know that if you have skills, you can jump right into the game and get to work.

THE BAD-"ISH"

Misconception #25: "You have to get certified to be a coach."

Nope. Not true. There is no organization that governs coaching certification schools, so anyone, yes anyone, can have a coaching school and offer a coaching certification. A brief Google search will show you just how many options you have.

When I started out, I thought I needed to be certified, so I paid $6,000 to go to a coaching school. It was many thousands of dollars more than I was comfortable paying at the time, but I figured the premium was worth having the certification stamp on my website. In all of my years as a coach, nobody has ever asked me about it. Not once. Did I learn some great things in the program? Yes, but does the certification itself mean anything in terms of getting clients? Not really.

Certification Madness

One of the illnesses that can afflict coaches while riding through the wild expanses of coachdom is called "certification madness." It's a common disease that tends to afflict new coaches. The symptoms often show up when a coach is new or is having a slump in her practice. When client enrollment is low, coaches often attempt to treat this problem with a misguided remedy: getting more training. While it's very attractive and will stop the symptoms for a while, certifications can become nothing more than a Band-Aid covering up the wound of self-doubt and the limiting belief that says, "I'm not enough." I'm not discounting continuing education. Rather I am asking you to check in on what is driving you to get more credentials.

In some coaching circles, I have seen certification madness grow like wildfire, infecting hundreds of coaches, with some coaches brandishing more than a dozen certifications on their websites, like Girl Scout badges.

Thomas, a talented young man I spoke with, had just completed his Master's in Psychology, as well as a coaching certification program. He called me to discuss doing another training program for $8,000. Over the phone I could tell he was showing signs of certification madness. I asked him a simple question, "What if tomorrow all new training was banned? And you had to build your whole career with the skills and experience you have right now? If I gave you five clients tomorrow, could you help them?" His answer was an excited "Yes!" Of course he could. He already had more skills and training than most coaches I have met.

If you are showing similar symptoms, ask yourself the same question. If someone referred me three new clients tomorrow, could I help them? If the answer is yes, get back to work, or enroll in a practice-building program for coaches. I know some good ones if you need a referral.

THE UGLY

Is It Gold Or Iron Pyrite?

With no barrier to entry, if you say you are a coach… you are. That means that there are people with a huge span of skill levels in this profession walking around with the same title: "Coach." Learning to discern who's a snake oil salesman and who's the real deal takes a bit of time, intuition and a good healthy dose of common sense.

In the days of the Gold Rush, many men went after what they thought was real gold, but it was actually iron pyrite (fool's gold). Later in the Gold Rush days, methods for separating real gold and fool's gold were developed and it was much easier to determine a false positive, to see if the ore you were panning was the real thing. In the coaching world, fool's gold generally falls under the category of what I call "hype-perbole."

"Hype-Perbole"

The actual word is hy·per·bo·le, but there is a lot of "hype" inherent in this noun. Here's the definition: Exaggerated statements or claims not meant to be taken literally.

Synonyms: exaggeration, overstatement, magnification, embroidery, embellishment, excess, overkill, rhetoric. Also includes bigger than life promises, usually around money; six figures this, seven figures that, promises of "massive transformation," "a new you," "radical change," etc. A general overuse of adjectives is common: Amazing! Remarkable! Astounding! Astonishing!

Now… I'm not a total motivational party pooper. There is nothing wrong with some good excitement to get people fired up, but… when we get so excited that we end up checking our brain at the door…. well… Houston, we have a problem.

Some Simple Rules to Keep You Away from Fool's Gold

• If it seems too good to be true... IT IS. Put your checkbook away, leave the pawnshop with the family silver and walk away.

• If your coach is constantly saying you are part of a select chosen few, know that you are likely not, no matter how flattering it feels.

• Avoid training programs with the word "Millionaire" in the title. They are usually run by people who are not, and filled with participants who will never be.

• If your coach can't provide you with references of past clients who thrived under their mentorship... Say goodbye, say goodbye to Hollywood.

The American Success Myth

"There are no shortcuts in life. Even though they are for sale everywhere."

– Dr. Logan

Overnight success is a myth. The coaching world is ripe with stories of rags to riches and overnight success, people who seemed to get "lucky." If you look deeper into every story of an overnight success, you will find at least a decade or two of hard work and persistence.

Enrollment vs. Manipulation

In coaching programs, techniques of "enrollment" are some of the first skills you will learn. Some of these techniques are actually straight-up manipulation. Manipulative enrollment techniques are so rampant in the industry that they have become assimilated into what's considered normal. "It's just business," they say. However you justify it, if what you are saying *is not true*, it is manipulation.

Here are some of the enrollment manipulation techniques I learned along the way. Sadly, some of these I originally used in my coaching practice, followed by varying degrees of discomfort and subsequent self-loathing.

Notice that most of these techniques speak directly to the small, insecure and scared part of us. They are not intended to connect with our higher selves.

Artificial Scarcity

You try to trick people into signing up by lying that you have a limited number of spaces left at your event or in your coaching practice. "Only two spots left!" When, in fact, you have plenty of spaces available…

Artificial Urgency

You attempt to create urgency by pretending to have a limited timeline. You send out emails telling people that they need to sign up NOW because the deadline is almost there, and the class will be *SOLD OUT if you wait!*

Success Inflation

It's the game that everybody in the industry is playing, but deep down nobody wants to look at. You talk about the one or two of your stand-out clients as if their success reflects the general results of your clients. You do things like casually drop public comments of having a "full practice" when you don't.

Fantastical Thinking Enabler

You promote what Dan Harris, author of the best-selling book *10% Happier,* calls a kind of "reckless hope," by focusing on getting clients to talk about their huge and totally unrealistic goals as a means of selling them coaching. What this person sitting in front of you really needs is a reality check, not someone to help perpetuate their patterns of fantastical thinking. "I want to buy an island like Richard Branson!" How about we focus on paying off your massive credit card debt and selling your extra cars?

False Exclusivity

You attempt to create exclusivity by creating perceived barriers to entry. For example, "we only accept a limited number of highly qualified individuals every year." When really, if you pass the basics and you can pay, then you are in.

One of the big challenges of the coaching world centers on this idea that in order to attract people to your events, you have to make them look exclusive. Like a nightclub owner making people wait outside, to create the illusion of popularity, coaches and the self-help industry, at large, seem to be addicted to this technique of creating false barriers to inclusion.

One of my all-time personal favorites is the "Invitation Only" event, where *everyone* is invited. (The most inclusive-exclusive event of all time!)

There Is Nothing Wrong With You

If you have had the feeling that there is incongruence between what coaches are saying versus the results their clients are getting, you are not alone. When I first started seeing this, I didn't want to look. I wanted to believe in the fantasy. I wanted to believe I could massively transform my life in a weekend seminar. I too could be making loads of cash in a very short period of time! Like an overweight person up for yet another crash diet program, I was sucked in by the fantasy. Sheer excitement had me ignoring the signs, so I second-guessed myself. When I didn't get the advertised results, I assumed there was something wrong with me. There was not.

If this feels familiar, just know there is nothing wrong with you either.

SELF HELP 101

WHY YOU SIGNED UP

WHAT REALLY HAPPENED

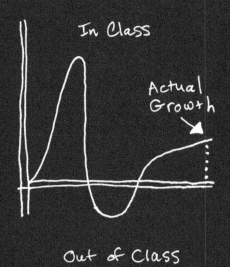

THE WAY THROUGH

"In coaching, there is a fine line between 'huckster of false hope' and 'inspired motivator.' It all comes down to honestly qualifying clients through the enrollment process."

– Dr. Logan

Clean Enrollment

Clean enrollment is not about getting people hyped up around their delusions of grandeur or capitalizing on their fears and greed. It's not about selling them on how great you are. Clean enrollment happens over time and through a process of connecting with what really matters to your client and finding their edge. Finding the place coach Brian Whetten calls both "scary and safe." It's about creating the space for your clients to give all of their fears — as well as their enthusiasm — a voice, so that you can honestly diagnose where you client is in their life and how big of a leap they will have to take to get to where they want to go.

Don't Be a Used Car Salesman

If you are calling yourself a successful coach, but are not truly living successfully in a way that matters to you, your clients won't succeed. If you are a health coach and secretly live an unhealthy life, it will show. I saw a beautifully done video by a coach online who discussed how to have money breakthroughs. The production value on the video was high and it was very inspiring at first look. However, I know that any client that works with him is not likely to have any major money breakthroughs, because I know this coach and he has been living paycheck to paycheck for years.

The great news is, if you are growing your coaching practice in an honest, authentic way, you will win in the long run. Who you choose to "be" in the world speaks louder than anything you say. Your personal integrity and honesty will always show up in the quality of your work and the people who are attracted to you. This level of authenticity is something that can't be faked. *You must walk your talk.*

"Busy-ness is laziness."

— Steve Chandler

LOVING TURTLES
& SALES CHICKENS

3

Slow Is the New Fast

t's easy to confuse movement with productivity.
Bouncing around like a jack rabbit on speed, tweeting,
updating your website, updating your profile,
organizing your desktop, you move faster and faster,
trying to outrun your fears.

This pace dehumanizes you, and turns you into a
coaching machine, scrambling around in a world where
you are always behind, trying to catch up. Socially you are
praised. "Oh you are very busy, you must be successful!"
But really, it's just a Band-Aid, moving you farther from
what you want… MORE CLIENTS.

One Client at a Time

I have found myself thinking, "I need X number of
clients" many times. It's a poisonous thought. If you are
thinking of potential clients as a number to fill, like a
quota, it is going to be hard to connect with the person
sitting right in front of you. The person that very well
MAY be your next client.

How do you fill a ten-person retreat? One person at a time.

How do you fill your coaching practice? One person at a time.

Your First *New York Times* Article

When meeting with a new potential client, I like to pretend that I have been assigned to write a front-page story about them for the *New York Times*. I have been given the valuable job of learning about the intimacies of their life, their dreams, their pains and what makes them tick. I come with a deep curiosity about this person and assume I know nothing.

Power Questions

• What do you want? What's in the way? What are you willing to give up to get it?

• If your life was a chapter in a book, what's the title of the chapter you have been living in? If you could choose a title for the next chapter of your life, what would you want it to be titled, and why?

• What's missing from having you feel like a whole person?

• What part of you is yearning to be expressed? (Especially if you don't feel like it's entirely appropriate and may stir up some trouble).

• In what ways are you still waiting to live?

• What outcome in your life would be worth $100,000 to you?

Raging Curiosity

What if this person you are going to meet was super important to you and your future? How would you treat your time together? For starters, you would Google him and read everything that has been written about him. You would scour his website and Facebook pages to learn everything you could. Now imagine how good that person is going to feel when he realizes how much personal interest you have taken in him. How much more effective will your session be because you will be asking questions coming from a place of informed curiosity?

"So you are saying you would spend hours researching someone before you meet him, then give him two hours of your time, all before he ever signed up to work with you?"

YES.

I love people. And I know that even if they never sign up for any of my programs, I will have fun getting to know them.

Nobody Wants a Coach/
Everybody Wants a Coach

Nobody wants a coach. They want the future version of themselves and the results they imagine they will get after working with you. Coaches have a tendency to get a bit too focused on themselves and feel they need to somehow prove themselves when meeting potential clients. Focus on the *client's future* and allow him to share his dreams with you. If you feel an impulse to talk about yourself, stop and ask yourself, "Where is this coming from?"

"Everything happens in your client's world, not yours."

— Steve Chandler (again)

Dani, a coach from San Francisco, was at the end of her initial session with Rhonda, a potential client who was not sure if she was ready for coaching. Dani brought up a story from Rhonda's blog that was particularly courageous. Rhonda immediately connected with the energy of the story. It was a story from a major high point in her life. "What would the you from that story have to say to the person who is sitting here right now?" Dani asked. "She would say, 'shit or get off the pot!'" "What would it be worth to you to get your best you back?" Dani asked. After a short pause Rhonda responded, "I can't believe you read that story." "I read your entire blog," Dani answered.

Rhonda signed up for coaching right there.

"People don't care how much you know, until they know how much you care."

— Theodore Roosevelt

60

Slow It Down to Turtle Speed

If you slow your busy self down, you will find that there are people and opportunities all around you. I find responding to people in person who sign up for my email list really wows them. Instead of spending all of my time focused on churning out endless content, I connect with the people who are reaching out to me. They are often shocked that I would take the time to speak with them because they signed up on my email list. They expect an auto responder-generated email, along with several well-crafted follow up emails. What they get instead is ME.

When someone new signs up for my mailing list, I get an email notification. Often I'll reach out, with a simple question.

"What brings you to me?"

If they sound interesting, I respond with "call me."

I have signed twelve-month coaching clients from the conversations that grew out of this simple connection and some genuine curiosity.

I find that people looking for coaches can show up as a bit timid sometimes. They hang out on the periphery. Reaching out to them brings them right into direct human connection, the thing they need the most.

Take It to the Streets

Why do we so often choose to speed up and get busy, rather than slow down and connect? One reason is that opening up our hearts to authentically connect with someone can be emotionally risky. It sets us up to feel disappointed or rejected if they say "no" to what we are offering. Instead of getting out there and talking to people, we hide out at home on our computers.

"THE MOST INTIMIDATING THING TO DO IS ALMOST ALWAYS THE MOST PRODUCTIVE."

Meeting people in person, speaking in person, is much more emotionally risky than chatting online. Because coaching is intimate in nature, if you want to sign people up, you have to go out and be with people. Or, as best-selling author Iyanla Vanzant said to a graduating class of Spiritual Psychology Master's students, "You now have the wisdom and the tools, it's time to *take it to the streets!*"

One way to jumpstart "taking it to the streets" is to ask yourself: "What would I do to connect with people if the Internet shut down tomorrow? How would I give people an experience of what I do? How would I be of service in a world without blogs, Instagram, Twitter, Facebook or email?"

I'M A CHICKEN
I'M SO AFRAID
BOO SALES
I'M SCARED
I'M A SALES CHICKEN
SALES IS SCARY

"Selling" for Sales Chickens

I'm a bona fide, card-carrying, sales chicken. When I feel like I'm selling something, my hands sweat, my voice cracks back to prepubescent tones and I start babbling nonsense in the hope you won't see the pee stain forming on the front of my pants. Even if you aren't as *fowl* as I am, here's a game changer that helped this sales chicken immensely.

I used to come into a session with a potential client with the intent to sell them, while simultaneously pretending I wasn't. I felt like a predator posing as a house pet, hanging out by the chicken coup. Sound familiar? A simple reframe turned that around for me. *Show up with the intention to SERVE, and nothing else.* When I come with the intention to be purely of service, magic happens; I feel calm, excited and in total integrity.

Don't Talk About Coaching

When you meet a potential client who wants to "talk to you about coaching," you don't want to do that. Talking about something is not service. Real service is coaching them right on the spot! Set up a meeting time in a private place, the quiet corner of a fancy hotel lounge, for example, or your office. Do not meet them at a coffee shop or other busy public place. When you set up the meeting, let them know that they will be coached and to come prepared.

How to Avoid Some Big No-No's

Potential Client: "Let's meet, I want to pick your brain."
You: "Ouch... I don't let people pick my brain. I do love coaching people, though. Would you like to meet and be coached?"

Potential Client: "Let me take you out to coffee."
You: "I don't do coffee, but if you want to meet for a coaching session, I'm in."

Request an Exchange

If you agree to waive your fee when you meet someone for an initial session, before they meet with you, request that they do something to earn the privilege of your time. I give potential clients homework *before we meet*. This is a great filter. If they don't complete the homework by the agreed upon time before your session, cancel the meeting. Let them know that *you will be available when they are ready to commit*. People want to be treated like adults. They crave someone in their lives to give them strong boundaries. Don't be afraid to lose potential clients. I have canceled sessions only to have clients come back to me months or years later, ready to work.

I also request that any person I talk to send me a follow-up "learning" email. I have them include their key learnings, breakthroughs, gratitude and any questions. This not only helps them anchor their learning, but it also helps me understand what they got out of the conversation, and it completes the cycle of exchange.

One caveat to not charging for your initial coaching session, is that by meeting with a potential client, make it clear that you are NOT giving them a "FREE" session.

Free is cheap. Free is junky. Free is the plastic Pokémon keychain you get with your $10 purchase at the gas station. This is about *service*. Coaching is your service to the world. Potential clients do homework for you, they show up ready to be coached and you coach them.

Charging for an Initial Session?

If the idea of waving your fee for the initial coaching session does not sit well with you, and you want to offer coaching packages rather than individual sessions like a therapist, you can charge for your initial session or sessions and then request that your clients make a bigger commitment if they want to go further with you. Some examples of fee structures:

• Offer three initial sessions for $275 each. After that, clients must commit to a minimum of six months of coaching if the relationship is a win-win.

• A single powerful session of three hours is $500, after that it's a commitment to be coached for at least one year.

Make it up, experiment — get creative.

"Be yourself, everyone else is already taken."

— **Oscar Wilde**

COACH
YOUR STORY

4

n my book, *Your Wild & Precious Life*, the opening sentence reads, "I believe we learn best through story."

This chapter opens with, "I believe we coach best through story."

I don't like pretending I have it all together. I'm uncomfortable telling an audience how to change their lives. I don't like the responsibility or imagined status that people project on me as someone who "knows THE ANSWER." I'm not and I don't. What I am is… open to learning, willing to continually experiment with my life and share it with others.

EXPERIMENT WITH YOUR LIFE!

~~THE ANSWER~~

Coach Your Story

"Give up defining yourself — to yourself or to others. You won't die. You will come to life. And don't be concerned with how others define you. When they define you, they are limiting themselves, so it's their problem. Whenever you interact with people, don't be there primarily as a function or a role, but as the field of conscious Presence. You can only lose something that you have, but you cannot lose something that you are."

— Eckhart Tolle

Share your story. Coach the way you want to be coached. Lead the retreats that you want to go on. Write the book that you want to read. Don't waste a single second wondering what the world needs or trying to guess what people want.

Do it for YOU.

WHAT CHANGED YOUR LIFE?

WHAT HURDLES HAVE YOU OVERCOME?

WHAT MISUNDERSTANDINGS ABOUT LIFE HAVE YOU CLARIFIED?

WERE YOU EVER TOTALLY BLINDSIDED BY LIFE?

WHAT ARE THE MAGICAL MOMENTS IN YOUR JOURNEY?

When you share *your story*, it gives people a chance to see a part of themselves in you. They feel a kinship and they trust you to lead them, because they know you have already been down the path they are on.

Life coach Martha Beck wrote a book about leaving the Mormon Church. She also wrote a book about her son with Down Syndrome. Neither of these books is about life coaching. But, guess what? At her life coaching events, I always run into Mormon women who have left the church and mothers with special needs children. She has a powerful story; these women see themselves in it and they are drawn to her.

If you are attracted to coaching and helping other people, my guess is that you have gone through at least one major life challenge, if not many. How you got through your challenges, and how you came out on the other side, is the gold in your story that will attract clients to you.

Show 'Em Your "Uglies"

"Why, when we know that there's no such thing as perfect, do most of us spend an incredible amount of time and energy trying to be everything to everyone? Is it that we really admire perfection? No — the truth is that we are actually drawn to people who are real and down-to-earth. We love authenticity and we know that life is messy and imperfect."

— Brené Brown

Hiring a coach is an inherently courageous act. It challenges us to expose the cracks in the well-shined armor of our outer personality. You cannot grow without exposing your vulnerabilities. As a coach, it's your responsibility to go first. If you want your clients to show you where they need help, model for them that being vulnerable is safe.

This is where coaching your story is so powerful. Share your story in all of its juicy dimensions. Tragedy and adversity foster connection. People love to connect with each other through their challenges, hardships and screw-ups.

MY
UGLIES

☆

When my first book came out, I celebrated the best year of my career as a coach. Ahhhh yes, I had made it! I had turned my passion into a lucrative career! I celebrated, I took four months off of work and I traveled. I bought a vintage trailer, and went to the Burning Man Festival. There I learned how to walk on stilts (a childhood dream) and even made it onto the front cover of the local newspaper.

Life was grand, until…

I discovered that I had *not* created an automatic money machine, but rather a coaching practice that needed my attention. Clients stopped calling and I was gifted a nice big piece of humble pie. From the day I started coaching, my business had more than doubled every year and now the magic had stopped. I was afraid to let anyone know what had happened for fear that I would somehow lose my reputation as a successful coach and entrepreneur. *The shame weighed heavily on me.*

Finally, things picked back up and rather than just pretend that I had been thriving the whole way through, I decided to follow my own advice and tell the whole story and "show 'em my uglies." I wrote a Facebook post that felt so vulnerable, I almost deleted it — twice. It read:

F*%K 2014

"2014... was one hell of a challenging year. My mother passed unexpectedly, my baby (who I love dearly) showed up in the world with all of the joy and sleeplessness that new parenting entails... After five years of living on the water, we were told our little home would be demolished to make way for an overpriced, big, shiny filing cabinet for professionals. I had to cancel my annual Nepal Adventure and my business went to sleep.

I prayed at the beginning of the year, something I only do when I really mean it. I prayed for a sign that we were on the right track. I said, "Show me a sign, something I can recognize." To be honest, I figured if something didn't change, I was ready to pack up the family, check out and go live on the beach in Costa Rica in a hut for a year and recover. Maybe sell coconuts or something..

And then... (drum roll)

The next morning after my prayer and just plain surrender, a new client showed up — and then another the next day. And then I got an offer to go to Hawaii to coach a client and play for a week! Wow! The next day, Alex, my lovely gal, got a call to start a new project with a company she has been wanting to work with for a long time.

***ALL in one week! OK… universe, God, whoever... I got the sign!!!! Thank you!

(I forgive myself for wanting to print and sell T-shirts that said "F*%K 2014")

Ah... it feels good to breathe again."

This post put me in deep connection and conversation with my people. It turned out I was not the only one who had a hard year, and this post gave people an open forum to comment and share about their own challenges.

"What is uttered from the heart alone, Will win the hearts of others to your own."

— Goethe

Let Your Freak Flag Fly!

"As we let our light shine, we unconsciously give other people permission to do the same. As we are liberated from our own fear, our presence actually liberates others."

— Marianne Williamson

From Wikipedia: **Freak Flag** — *To behave in an unconventional or unrestrained manner; to exhibit the uninhibited side of one's personality.*

Lead with your uniqueness and idiosyncrasies. All of us have things that make us different, strange and weird. Most people, except those very close to us, never get to see those delicious parts. Take a risk and lead with that side of you that few get to see.

James Stein is a storyteller, a motivational speaker, business consultant and a self-made web celebrity. He shared a story with me about a recent consulting job. "The company I was working with was full of all these old-school corporate types, dressed in blue blazers and loafers. The guy who hired me asked me to start coming into board meetings with the top management. I asked him, 'Do I need to clean up my act,' pointing to my pink hair and facial jewelry. 'No!' he responded, 'I want you to come in just like you are. Let them get curious.'

Months later he told me he's now in charge of meetings with the company staff. He leads daily gratitude circles and opens them up for intimate levels of sharing that are way beyond the usual decorum of a corporate environment. At the end of the call he paused and said to me, "I love you." I paused for a second. I didn't expect that. Then I hear myself say, "I love you too." And I hung up. A huge smile comes across my face. This man really means it. He is walking his talk, flying his freak flag and making a huge difference while he does it.

YOUR PERSONAL FREAK FLAG

Your quirks + your strange hobbies + your favorite rules to break + stuff you do when nobody is around + secret obsessions + your potty mouth + your pink hair + the super hero you wish you were + your unconventional beliefs. = Your Freak Flag

My Personal Freak Flag

I'm a stilt-walking, tutu-wearing, obsessive heirloom tomato growing, rule-breaking, random act of kindness doing, sometimes F-bomb dropping (sorry, Mom), medicine journeying, Spiritual Psychology Master's degree having, Corporate America drop-out who loves setting people free, connecting people with their hearts and bringing highly effective woo-woo to the entrepreneurial change-makers of this world.

THE COACH'S JOURNEY

COMFORT ZONE
1

THE CALL
2

THE JOURNEY BEGINS
3

COMMITMENT
4

DARK NIGHT OF THE SOUL
5

TRIALS & TRIBULATIONS
6

SURRENDER
7

A MENTOR APPEARS
8

INTEGRATE & TAKE ACTION
9

RETURN HOME TRIUMPHANT
10

The Coach's Journey:

Stage 1 — **Comfort Zone** — Something needs to change, there must be more to life!

Stage 2 — **The Call** — I see a vision for the future, but I'm scared to act on it.

Stage 3 — **The Journey Begins** — I leave my comfort zone.

Stage 4 — **Commitment** — There is no turning back. I'm all in.

Stage 5 — **Dark Night of the Soul** — What did I do? I can't do this! I made a mistake.

Stage 6 — **Trials & Tribulations** — I use familiar strategies expecting a different result.

Stage 7 — **Surrender** — I eat humble pie. I admit I am lost. Some part of me must die.

Stage 8 — **A Mentor Appears** — I am ready to learn new ways of being.

Stage 9 — **Integrate & Take Action** — I turn my news ways of being into new ways of acting.

Stage 10 — **Return Home Triumphant** — I share my learning with my people.

The Coach's Journey — The Hero's Journey

"The Hero's Journey," popularized by the American Mythologist Joseph Campbell, was the inspiration for George Lucas's original Star Wars trilogy. It's also a useful roadmap for personal growth. It's the journey that we all take when we choose to leave behind what is familiar for the hope of something new. Campbell's map gives insight into our inner and outer processes and is a great framework to help you see the mythological arc of your own story.

Where are you on your Hero's Journey?

Maybe you have already returned home?

Maybe you are still out on your adventure?

What's your next move?

For a detailed version of my personal hero's journey, see my book *Your Wild & Precious Life: Adventures in Conscious Creation*.

Sharing Your Story Online

When telling your narrative in an honest, open way, you are allowing people to see a full range of your humanity. Your people get to come along on the journey with you, with all of its ups and downs and messy humanness. You are giving them a back stage peek into your personal evolution.

When you focus on cultivating an image, you are effectively alienating yourself and others from having a true experience of who you are.

"Don't think of your website as a self-promotion machine, think of it as a self-invention machine. Online, you can become the person you really want to be. Fill your website with your work and your ideas and the stuff you care about."

— Austin Kleon

"There is no shortage of suffering and unfulfilled dreams on this planet. Which means that there is no limit to the number of people you can help. Anyone and everyone could benefit from some coaching in their lives."

– Brian Whetten, Ph.D

I Need More Clients!

This chapter is not about "getting clients," because they are not fish that can be caught. This chapter is a collection of non-traditional ways of "creating" clients through your acts of service, love, play and creativity. If you have an artistic, spontaneous, rebellious streak (like me), and the idea of promoting your coaching practice in a linear, business-centric write your blog, build your list and market yourself kind of way feels like poison to your soul... don't worry, we are not going to do that.

Clients Come from the Darnedest Places!

"Mommy, where do clients come from?" The correct answer is: "They come from everywhere!"

8 FUN WAYS TO CREATE CLIENTS

1. VOLUNTEER

I volunteered as a core staff member of a fundraiser called Spirit Walk. I put time, energy and heart into it. Every year, people I met through this experience ended up coming on my retreats.

2. PLAY

I joined a Burning Man camp and led a 40-minute guided meditation for the members of the camp as a gift. They loved it. Several of them became clients.

3. WRITE A HANDWRITTEN LETTER

Three years after an introductory coaching session with a young woman, I wrote her a letter asking how she was doing on the goals we talked about. She shared that our session opened her heart to the possibility of a different future, but she got scared and never called me back. The handwritten letter opened up our conversation again and she became a client.

4. DO PRO BONO WORK

I spent several hours coaching a young man who was in trouble, who did not have a penny to his name. I didn't ask for an exchange of any kind, nor did I expect I'd ever hear from him again. Two months later, he referred me to a paying client that worked with me for two years.

5. COACH SOMETHING ELSE

I work as a TED speaker coach. This is a volunteer position that requires a lot of work and dedication. I do it because I love helping people craft their message and it affords me the unique opportunity to work intimately with all kinds of interesting and talented people. I don't coach for TED *because* it helps me get new clients. That came as an unexpected benefit. My TED clients refer me coaching clients as well as private clients who need help with speeches.

6. LEARN A NEW SKILL

I learned how to lead breathwork meditation circles and expanded my coaching practice to include bi-monthly live events and telephone meditation circles that have also landed me several corporate meditation and wellness contracts.

7. OFFER A CLASS AS A GIFT

I offered a class as a gift to the participants at a bi-annual coaching conference. I was not on the roster as a speaker or as a workshop leader. I advertised with a handwritten sign and used an empty room without furniture. I did it on a whim, because there was nobody at the event offering anything like what I had to offer. I did it out of service, without any expectation of how many people would show up. I ended up with wait lists for my classes. Who knew? I sure had no idea how popular they would be. People from those classes have gone on my retreats and continue to be involved in my work.

8. HAVE FUN WITH OPPOSITES

One method to create clients is to bring your work to communities that you find inspiring or captivating and see if you can offer anything as a yin to the communities natural yang. If you know a very serious group, bring some play to their world. If it's a group made up mostly of women and you are a man, join in and bring your masculine presence and point of view.

Twice a year, I am hired to lead a breathwork meditation for the leadership team of "million dollar producers" for a multi-national health products company. These folks mean business and I love bringing some woo-woo into their lives. Would I ever have guessed they would be open to this work? No. But, I shared my work with their leader and she took a risk to offer up something out of the ordinary to her team. It turns out that they love it!

Take Your Clients Into the Wild

One of the most powerful things you can do is to take your clients out of their environment and get them into nature. An entire branch of therapy has evolved from research done on using nature as a catalyst for change.

Craig Chalquist, the author of *Ecotherapy*, shares:

"Most clients don't realize that much of the grief, shame, emptiness, and fear they struggle with may be a natural response to the unnatural way we live.

"The problem of our day is an inner deadening, an increasingly deployed defense against the stresses of living in an overbuilt industrialized civilization saturated by intrusive advertising and media, unregulated toxic chemicals, unhealthy food, parasitic business practices, time-stressed living, and (in the United States) a heart-warping culture of perpetual war and relentlessly, mindless political propaganda.

"Reconnection with nature and one's own body; working with our plant and animal friends; voluntary simplicity; detaching from rigidly artificial time schedules; changing home or work environments; (doing) dream therapy focusing on individual or collective dreams about nature; wilderness retreats; environmental activism; healing spiritual practices; and recovery from compulsive consumerism...

"These things are so needed because in our highly mechanized society, humans are more and more being treated like machines. I contend that symptoms and conflicts occur because human beings are not machines. We have evolved a wide variety of ways of relating to our world. We are sensual, curious, and creative. Most of all, we are soft, protean, organic beings, not mechanical components."

Take your clients out to nature and watch them thrive. Watch as the environment *magnifies* the coaching you do with your clients.

Wow Your Clients

New clients come from existing clients. Make their experience life-changing and they will fill your programs for you. Remember that your clients will expect to get what they paid for: X number of sessions, a certain number of in-person meetings, etc. If you really want to be of service to them, surprise them with additional, thoughtful, meaningful and fun offerings. Be generous. *This is only limited by your creativity.*

• **Send a book, a movie or article** — If you see something you know your client will get a lot out of, send it to them. Get an Amazon Prime account and you can send books in two days with no shipping charges.

• **Help them be healthy** — If your client wants to work out and is struggling, surprise him and invite him to a workout session. I once called a client who was struggling to get back into running and said, "Show up to our next meeting in your running gear. We can have your session another time — this one is on me." We went for a very hard run. He later shared it was the best thing

I ever did for him as his coach. I not only stretched him and moved him into action, but it showed him how much I cared.

• **Take a class with your client** — Rochelle, a coach in Santa Monica, took her client to a wonderful three-day workshop, because she knew her client would not go alone and it was exactly what he needed. (Rochelle paid for her own $400 entrance fee.) Her client was wowed!

• **Offer an extended session** — When your client really needs some extra TLC, offer them a two- to three-hour session as a gift from you. They will love it.

• **Tell Your Clients Your Truth** — Nothing creates lifelong fans like having a straight-up honest relationship with your clients. Get their permission, and then tell them how you experience them. Tell them your truth. Even if it may be upsetting, tell them anyway. They are not paying you to be their friend; they are paying you to coach them.

Narrow Their Options

You can be anything you want to be! If you can dream it, you can create it! These are the dominant motivational mantras. While exciting and fun, they can also be profoundly paralyzing. I once heard a young guy describe himself as a possibilitarian, living wild and free, hooked on the narcotic fantasy of endless options. I also noted that he was struggling financially because he had spent so much time in the land of infinite possibility, he hadn't really planted himself long enough to create anything of substance. His self-described "freedom" looked more like avoidance of commitment gleefully disguised as adventure.

"If everything is an option, then nothing is an option."

— Anonymous

People thrive with limits. Barriers, ceilings, walls and rules all support us in growing. Even if you like to break the rules and bust the barriers, that's great! But know, without them you are lost, like an explorer walking across the Arctic tundra without a compass. If you have a wandering client who seems lost, help them find their way by limiting their possibilities and narrowing their options. From my own experience as a wandering soul, I can tell you that finding my path has been a steady process of experimentation and elimination. Some of the best coaching I ever received smacked me right out of "Possibility Never Never Land" and into making choices and sticking to them.

Stay Focused on Service

If you want to create clients, you must be focused on serving them. You can't be focused on yourself and others at the same time. It's one or the other. Anytime you find yourself in fear or stressed about getting clients, it's because you are in the "me" mode. How do you get out? Jump back over to service. When you are focused on doing something for others, your fears and worry will fade into the creativity and inherent joy found in service.

"You don't get paid what you deserve. You get paid what you negotiate."

– Dalai Mama

When I worked in the insurance industry, I was very good at making money. The system of payment and all of the rules around it were pre-set and all I had to do was learn how to constantly get better at operating in that system.

When I left the corporate world and went out on my own as a coach, all kinds of money conversations showed up that I never had to deal with as an employee. Suddenly I was selling myself — I became the product. It brought up all kinds of self-esteem issues and confusion around pricing, the value of my services and my own value as a coach. I also had this idea that money somehow corrupted the purity of my new "noble" work. I just wanted to help people and not have to deal with all the money stuff!

In this chapter we will explore some fun ways to make money as a coach. We will dive into the most powerful learning that helped me untangle my misunderstandings around money that kept me from being a prosperous coach.

"You are not your job.
You are not how much money you have in the bank.
You are not the car you drive.
You are not the contents of your wallet.
You are not your fucking Khakis."

— Tyler Durdan, *Fight Club*

You Are Not What You Charge

A major misconception for coaches and for all kinds of service-based entrepreneurs is the belief that you are what you charge. *You are not.* I see coaches who charge high fees walk around wearing their fees around their necks like a dangling piece of temporary self-esteem enhancing bling. They make sure everyone in their circles knows how much they earn. While lower-earning coaches feel shame, like they should be wearing a scarlet letter.

On the extremes, you may be excellent at enrolling people in your programs but you might not be that great of a coach. You could also be a very skilled coach who is a horrific sales chicken. Just because you have five clients each paying you $20,000 to coach them, does not make you a $20,000 coach. All it says is that five people have agreed to pay you $20,000 for coaching.

On the flip side, if you charge $75 for a session, it does not mean you are a $75 coach. All it means is that currently people are paying you $75 to coach with you. I have seen coaches (including myself) shift from charging $100 a session to charging $10,000 for a package in the same month. Did we suddenly become more worthy, more skilled coaches overnight? NO. We just made a different offer, someone agreed and we stepped up to the challenge. (I'm simplifying here.)

How Much Do I Charge?

New coaches always stress about their fees. Oh, lets be honest… every coach stresses about their fees at some point. Coaches want to know, "How much do I charge?" Here is the secret: *It doesn't matter. There are no rules.* How much you charge is just an agreement between you and the client. It's an exchange. You could have every single one of your clients on a different coaching package, all paying different rates.

I used to have this nightmare that my clients would all somehow find each other and compare rates and then they would stage an intervention and all circle up in my living room demanding an explanation. Of course this was just reflective of my own unresolved issues around the flexibility of money and what it meant to create different levels of value with my clients.

On the extreme end of woo-woo land, I know an intuitive coach that sets his rate based on his read of how much energy he is going to have to expend holding space for his client and their vision. It's a "pay by the psychic pound" pricing strategy!

One of the things I work on with coaches is learning to loosen up their relationship with money so that they can experience more financial freedom and flexibility in their work.

Here's an example of how this flexible money thing

operates in the real world and why you don't have to worry about an imaginary client intervention session if you decide to play with your rates: when you fly on an airplane you know that the other passengers have paid different prices to get to the same place. On any given flight there are at least six to ten different rates passengers pay to get to the SAME PLACE. Some signed up early, some paid with a special card, and some are sitting in better seats. Nobody throws a tantrum on the plane because they paid more than the guy sitting next to them. It's just understood and accepted. Coaching is the same. It's your airplane. YOU CAN CHARGE WHATEVER YOU WANT.

Have fun with this, loosen up, BREATHE and experiment!

COACH AIRLINES

WE CHARGE WHAT WE WANT.
ALWAYS.

An Experiment...

I spoke with Lane, a young, talented artist who wanted me to coach him to expand his business. He was a big "yes!" for me as a potential client. He was very coachable, enthusiastic, and had a track record of following through. There was one challenge that I could not overlook. He had a sizable debt. He shared with me that he had no hesitation to put a year of coaching with me on a credit card. I learned that most of his debt was from personal growth programs, so I told him if he wanted to work with me, he would have to start paying down his debt and pay for our work in cash.

I challenged him to pay off 10% of his debt in sixty days. I said I would waive my minimum commitment of a year if he succeeded, and he could hire me month by month, as long as he continued to pay down his debt. Two months later he called me to share that he had fallen short of our goal, but had managed to save several thousand dollars towards his debt, which was a huge deal for him! He got a tiny taste of what was possible.

I could have allowed him to pay me with a credit card. You could say I lost $10,000. But I get to sleep at night. I don't believe in deficit spending. I don't promote it, even if it would benefit me financially, even if the client thinks that our work together could pull them out of their financial rut. This kind of "gambler's mindset" can lead to the "I'll win my money back" syndrome that bankrupts so many people in Las Vegas and personal growth circles alike.

Some day, down the road when his debt is paid off, I might just get a call from someone who is ready to do the work and pay for it in earned money, instead of unearned, extended hope.

What's Worthiness Got to Do with It?

During a coaching call with a client, he shared with me that he felt that his inability to charge a good rate as a coach was based on not feeling worthy of receiving payment for his work. He was very successful in the publishing industry but felt insecure about his work as a coach. "You know," he said, "I just have to work on this worthiness thing and I think *then* I will feel ready to get paid what I deserve."

My response: "You don't get paid what you deserve. You get paid what you negotiate."

There was a long pause.

"Can you explain?" He asked.

"You don't get paid what you *deserve*. You get paid what you negotiate.

"It's not like there is a big empty 'deservability' jar and once it fills up, then you start charging for your services. The first time I offered a higher rate for a year of coaching, it was not because my jar was full. Somebody else, my coach, believed in me and said, 'you should be charging more.' My mother said... 'you should be charging more.' So... I had two people pushing me to step up my game."

When the next potential client asked my rate, I said, "$10,000 for a year of coaching." There was a long pause.

DESERVABILITY

My hands dripped with sweat and my knee started to tap without my permission. Luckily, we were on the phone. "I'm in," he said. Two days later the check arrived. Two weeks later, another new client showed up and another $10,000 check arrived. I did a big happy dance around the living room. The following morning, I woke up in a cold sweat when I realized that I had two clients who were really vested and ready to play big. I knew I had to step up my game… and I did!

The pressure to perform pushed me to grow as a coach and my clients came with me. I took the risk to leap out ahead of my comfort zone and my feelings of "worthiness" as a coach, and was rewarded for my boldness. You could spend an entire lifetime working on your "worthiness and money issues," or you could take a risk and raise your rates. *Offer it to the next potential client you meet.* They may surprise you and say "yes!" If not, then do it again. Keep doing it until someone says "sign me up."

Co-Creating Value

You may have noticed there is a lot of talk regarding the value of certain workshops, coaching programs and classes. Often it sounds something like this:

"Sign up for this program right now and get this workshop valued at $1,000 for free!"

Who sets the value? Who says it's worth $1,000?

Assuming ability on both the part of the coach and client, the value of a coaching agreement has three main pieces:

$$VALUE = THE\ COACH'S\ COMMITMENT + FIT + CLIENT'S\ COMMITMENT.$$

When we think of creating value *for* clients, we should really be thinking of it as co-creation; the value is created by both the coach and the client. If a client pays $5,000 to work with you but is not really committed to doing the work, it's not really worth $5,000 — no matter how good a coach you are. Similarly, if you are not committed to your client, the value of your work together is much less.

So if the value of coaching lies in the hands of both the coach and the client. How do I know what the value is so I can set my pricing?

We are back to the "What do I charge?" question again!

The best way I know how to do this is through what I call the 5x model. If your rate is $20,000 for a year, for example, then you want to help the client define goals that create a value that exceeds what they are paying you. I have clients imagine outcomes that are worth five times what they are paying for coaching. So in your case, have clients find an outcome that would be worth $100,000.

Your Fee x 5 = Your Client's Goal

When talking with a client I look for inner and outer goals that are both exciting to *them and me*. If I'm not excited about what they are doing and I don't feel the hair raise up on my arms or my intuition doesn't light up, I redirect them to look deeper and see what's below the surface. And we keep looking until we find it, or we don't work together.

The nice thing about the 5x model is, even if they only achieve 50% of their goal, they have still more than doubled their investment.

The Value Conversation

If your client's goals are mostly internal and have nothing to do with financial success, it's vital that you help your client assign dollar values to their intended outcomes. The operative question is, "What would that be worth to you?"

Recently, a client told me after five months of coaching, that he had already recouped his $10,000 investment. "How did you come to that assessment?" I asked. He then went into a detailed explanation of the shifts in his life he had made and how they had affected his life in a way that related to the money he spent. I felt a huge sigh of relief wash over me when he shared this. I had no idea he was getting so much benefit from our work together! I had threatened to fire him months before, because I was feeling like he was not committed to coaching. Ha! I was so wrong. Have the value conversation with your clients at least once a month. *This will help you co-create exceptional value.*

Another way to think about the value of your work as a coach is to remember this: Any changes the client makes on the inside, they get to keep for life. Once you have a shift of consciousness, it never goes away.

If your client shifts their internal conversation about money by 10% while working with you, that shift is amortized over the rest of their life. Imagine you help your client make a change that results in them consistently feeling 20% happier. What's the value of that spread out over forty more years of living? The answer is... A LOT!

I Will Not Under-Serve You

I met with a potential client who had some big goals. We had a powerful two-hour initial session and at the end I offered him a year of coaching. He asked me, "Don't you offer smaller packages?" I responded, "Yes, on rare occasions I do, and that's not what I am offering you, because it won't get you to where you want to go."

He declined the offer and I was fine with his choice.

Why didn't I negotiate with him? *I didn't want to under-serve him.* I knew he had a popular blog, plenty of clients and led workshops. I also knew he was afraid to charge good money for his work. My sense was that he would have to commit to himself in a much bigger way than he had before, and pay a solid fee for it, before he ever got over his own limitations around money.

Getting Paid to Do What You Love

Move beyond the basic "therapy model" of coaching. Take those coaching tools and do something creative with them! Do something that lights you up. Combine your coaching with things you love to do.

WHAT I LOVE TO DO
+ WHERE I LOVE TO DO IT
+ MY COACHING TOOLS
= CREATIVE COACHING IN ACTION

• **Stacey Warner & Katie Neligan** do Equus coaching at a horse ranch in Malibu. Their clients get coached while in the ring with the horses. Stacey also runs Mystic Cowgirl Retreats, where her clients do deep personal work and ride horses on the beaches of Costa Rica.

- I took a very athletic client stand up paddle boarding for a one-on-one adventure coaching session.

- Artist/Coach **Helen Bradley** takes people on healing journeys through expressive art in her studio in Los Angeles.

- **Jane Walker** uses her coaching and psychic abilities to coach people by connecting them with their ancestors as a resource for guidance and healing.

- I took a family to the jungles and mountains of Guatemala for a private ten-day transformational vacation.

- **Rhonda Linde** does sexuality coaching. She gets her clients out of the chair, out of their heads and onto the floor, using what she calls the wheel of healing. Her clients use their body and movement to heal issues around sex and sexuality.

- **Michael Trotta** is a nature-based coach that takes clients into the woods and uses Native American based mythology and wilderness skills to help people connect to their original medicine.

IF I COULD BE PAID TO TRAVEL ANYWHERE IN THE WORLD TO COACH PEOPLE IT WOULD BE

_____

IF I COULD COMBINE MY COACHING WITH ANY ACTIVITY IT WOULD BE _____

NOW COMBINE THEM...

IF I COULD GET PAID TO COACH PEOPLE WHILE _____, WHILE TRAVELING TO _____, THAT WOULD BE A DREAM!

It doesn't have to be a dream. It can be reality. That's how I started my business. At one point in my life, my favorite place to go was Baja Mexico and I loved kayaking. My first Insight Adventures™ retreat was a kayaking trip in Baja. This grew to desert retreats and international retreats to Nepal, Peru and Guatemala.

One of the ways I work with coaches is helping them transition to making their businesses more fun and adventurous. I also work with coaches to launch their first international retreats and make existing ones more impactful and lucrative.

"All work and no play, makes Jack a shitty coach."

– Dr. Logan

Y ou will spend most of your coaching career focused on your clients and their success. This chapter is all about YOU, Coach.

One day, when I was feeling especially stressed, I went out to surf to clear my head. While bobbing around in the water, waiting for the waves that were virtually non-existent that day, I remembered hearing that Angelina Jolie used underwater scream therapy. I was already out in the water, so I figured I would give it a shot. I slid off my board, and swam down five feet underwater. I peered around to make sure nobody was watching. Kind of ridiculous, I know, but nevertheless I had to look. No fish or people were onto me, so I let out a scream, "Ahhhh!" (Or what ever that sounds like underwater.)

I did it again, this time with full force, "AHHHHH"!!! I threw in some swearing to really make it count. Two stingrays darted off, leaving some puffs of sand. I apologized to them in my mind. Again, totally ridiculous, I know, but I was raised to be considerate. I couldn't help it. Out of air, I swam back to the surface and scanned the faces of the other surfers looking for a sign that they might have heard me. The coast was clear. I dove underwater again and let out a huge "roar!" When I broke the surface the second time, I could feel that all my upset was gone. I felt free. It had worked!

Why am I sharing this with you? Not just because I found screaming underwater to be an awesome off-the-wall way to release stress, but because I believe too many coaching books focus on goal line achievements and gloss right over the challenging parts of being a coach. Knowing how to take care of yourself is as important as taking care of your clients.

Self-care is the bedrock of any kind of transformational work. Without it, you inhibit your growth, cut off access to your intuition and ultimately burn out through unsustainable over-giving. One of my mentors calls it "Give-Give-Give Give UP!

Karmic Sherpa

Coaching is not therapy. However, if you work with someone over time, you will get to know them intimately and inevitably their deep personal issues will show up. I have often found myself thinking about my clients into the wee hours of the night. You may have experienced this as well. When you find yourself hauling around your client's challenges on your back like a Sherpa in Nepal, you have become what I call a Karmic Sherpa. In psychology this is called enmeshment.

Left unchecked, enmeshment drains your energy and leaves you increasingly less able to help your clients. A coach friend of mine says that she knows she's in trouble when she finds herself wanting things for her clients more than they do. "It's like pulling a legless donkey up hill!"

THE OVER-RESPONSIBILITY MANTRA

I am not responsible for other people's feelings.

I am not responsible for other people's healings.

I am not responsible for other people's interpretations of my words or actions.

I release myself from any false belief that I am personally responsible for my client's growth or outcomes.

Mourn Your Failures and Make Space

I know that in "self-help speak" there are no failures, only "learning opportunities." Yes, this is true in the highest sense, but this is also a very mental statement that can lead you to bypass your unresolved feelings. A bypass is what happens when we ignore our fears, doubts and failures and attempt to jump over them with spiritual explanations or manic enthusiasm.

The danger in a bypass is that you try to move forward without healing the wounds from the last time (or the last eight times) you tried something. All of the emotional baggage, lingering disappointment and judgments are still there, frozen in time, waiting to spring back to life once you hit your first challenge or the initial high from a new endeavor wears off.

It's the same thing that happens to people in relationships. They break up with someone, carrying a list of reasons why it didn't work out, and then they find someone new and the whole process starts over again.

Self-Forgiveness and Releasing Judgments

If there is one skill I want you to walk away with after reading this book, it's self-forgiveness. Self-forgiveness is a master skill in the toolbox of a highly effective coach. I use it every day.

Underneath every lingering upset is a judgment or a string of judgments. Those judgments you hold about yourself and the people around you are the glue that keeps your challenges and upsets firmly in place.

It works like this: You decide to take your coaching practice to the next level. You set some lofty goals, commit to working with a business coach and you are off and running. A month into creating your new vision, resistance shows up in a big way. All kinds of insecurities start popping up that you have not had to deal with in years. "I thought I healed this stuff!" you exclaim. "Why are all of these thoughts coming to haunt me as I'm trying to step up my game and make a bigger difference in the world? Ugggh!!! "

Here's what's happening: All of the unresolved material that has kept you at your current level of success is coming up to be healed. Hooray! So much fun! Left unhealed, it will function like driving your car around with the emergency brake on. No matter how much you put the pedal to the metal, you are not going to get out of third gear.

The good news is, there is a proven way to move through this mental and emotional onslaught. Underneath those thoughts and feelings there is a long list of judgments. Some of my personal all-time favorites include:

I judge myself as not ready.
I judge myself as not being clear on my big vision.
I judge myself having to sell out in order to grow my business.
I judge myself as a lame public speaker.
I judge myself as a big fat sales chicken.
I judge myself as too creative for business.
I judge myself to be in the wrong profession! Ha!

I call this the **"Self-Flagellation Merry-Go-Round."**

Move into Self-Compassion

If you can start to find self-compassion inside this list of judgments and begin to dissolve them from your consciousness, you have a chance of releasing the emergency brake. The tricky thing with judgments is, if you are experiencing them, it's because you created them. They don't come from anywhere else. I know it's popular to think that it's other people's judgments of us that are oppressive, but it's just not true. Since we are the ones creating the judgments that hurt us, wouldn't it make sense that we are the only ones who can release them? Bingo! *That's why spending your time trying to get others to stop judging you or having someone else absolve you of your negative beliefs about yourself is a total waste of time.

Close your eyes, put your hands over your heart and say, "I forgive myself for judging myself as _____." Move through your list of judgments. It may feel like a mental process in the beginning, but if you stay with it, emotions will start to bubble up around a specific judgment. *Maybe the one about feeling like you are not enough.* (Just a guess.) When this happens you know you have hit "self-forgiveness pay dirt." Repeat your self-forgiveness until you feel some relief.

Note: You are forgiving yourself for the judgment, *not* the action. You can't forgive an action. Actions are neutral. The only thing you can forgive is the *judgment that you placed on the action or experience.*

Judgments can be sticky, especially if you have been carrying them inside yourself for a long time. Some judgments will release the very first time you say, "I forgive myself," especially if you really mean it and feel strongly connected to your emotions in that moment. With other judgments, you may have to forgive yourself a thousand times before the whole thing lets go. We are not looking for perfection here, just progress.

Breathwork — The Power Tool to Consciousness

If you are like me, you hold your stress in your body. And it will often let you know exactly what is going on. Attempting to remove this stress through mental gymnastics like positive thinking, mantras or reframing is futile. Doing something physical, like going for a run, usually works well, but not completely.

My personal silver bullet for stress is Pranayama yoga breathing, or breathwork. Breathwork is a simple but powerful meditation that uses conscious breathing to activate your parasympathetic nervous system, reducing stress, inducing states of euphoria, mythopoetic imagery and inner peace. I mean, *who doesn't want that?!*

Most meditation practices are passive and require a lot of practice to master. Breathwork is so easy a three-year-old could do it. This is good news for me because I'm profoundly mediocre at all other kinds of meditation. I usually tell people, "I'm a meditation teacher who isn't any good at meditation. Welcome to my class!"

Breathwork has worked for me since day one and continues to be a highly effective practice that I use in my personal life and professional work.

My favorite story about using this meditation technique happened in the Hong Kong airport. I missed my flight to Nepal and was set to arrive the night before my clients showed up for a two-week retreat. My preparation time had been cut in half and I was mentally bashing myself for being so irresponsible. Desperate to get off the mental self-flagellation merry-go-round, I rented a tiny little shoebox of a room at the airport hotel to see if I could change my mood. In no time, I slipped into a deep trancelike state and two hours passed in what felt like minutes. I left my room feeling like I was walking on clouds. Everyone in the airport was beautiful to me, my stress was gone and my judgments dissolved. I arrived in Kathmandu rested, happy and ready to lead.

You can learn more about breathwork on my website: www.jessegros.com and download your complimentary breathing session.

Take a Trip Down Memory Lane

Have you ever heard the expression, "Don't take your hobby and make it a career, because you will soon stop liking your hobby"? There is truth to this saying, but it doesn't *have to be* true. How you relate to *yourself* as you go through the process of growing your business is what really matters. If you have workaholic tendencies, for example, they tend to come with you no matter what career you choose.

If you ever find yourself losing some of that original zest for your coaching career, (as I did) take a trip down Memory Lane and revisit your initial reasons and motivations for becoming a coach. I found that looking back at my writings, client emails, applications to coaching programs, etc., revealed a treasure trove of optimism, creativity and energy that I could connect with and use to reenergize myself.

Be Like Dicky —
A True Story about Learning to Receive

Dicky did something that had never been done before. He went to Burning Man and put himself inside a Plexiglas home for a week without supplies. He was totally dependent on the help of people outside his little home for food, personal waste removal and entertainment. It was a risk, and he didn't know how it would work out. He didn't know if people would help, or just hang out and harass him. He took a week-long deep dive into RECEIVING. It worked out well for him, people came all week long to read to him, feed him meals, carry away his waste and sing to him. They showed up in grand support.

How good are you at asking others for help? How good are you at receiving? Take a risk and BE LIKE DICKY.

Coaching Changes Lives

This is an excerpt from a client thank you letter that puts a smile on my face every time I read it. When things get challenging, I read it and I am reminded why I coach.

Hi Jesse,

I've been meaning to write you for weeks now. But every time I start writing, my words seem woefully inadequate to express my gratitude for your help last year. So I end up deleting my email and thinking that the right words will come. Maybe there aren't right words. So here goes...

Reaching out to you was one of the greatest things I've ever done for myself. It's funny how random things that you said on our calls — things I thought I heard but must not have fully understood — have come to me recently and brought with them entirely new levels of meaning. You saying, "Have fun with [the process]" was the best advice I received. Your hope and positivity helped me immensely. I can't tell you how much relief I felt just hearing you say that everything was okay — and mean it.

Today, I am the happiest that I've ever been — and I'm having the most fun of my life. Gavin and I have a wonderful marriage — we now know that our wedding was a gift. Through that experience, we created the space we wanted to find our best selves and bring those into our relationship. And we are so much better for it. We still have some things to work through with family members — old fears and letting go of the need for approval — but things seem to be flowing in a much more positive direction. You were right. We were on the precipice of a really magical transformation. And our lives today look nothing like they did...

Love, Erica

"There are no shortcuts in evolution."

– Louis D. Brandeis

Y ou can't build a sustainable coaching career in seven days, a month or even a year for that matter. It takes dedication, experimentation and a willingness to continually let go of what has worked in the past, so that you can discover the mystery waiting for you just around the next corner. In order to keep growing, you must EVOLVE.

You Are a Coach When You Have One

One of the things that most unsuccessful coaches have in common is that *they don't have one*. This was definitely my story for the first two years of my coaching practice. I had this egotistical idea that I did not need a coach to help me get my business off the ground. I figured I would just do it myself! (What a funny thing, to not use the service you offer.) I had my reasons why I didn't need a coach and they turned out to be the same reasons that people gave me about why they didn't want to work with me. "Why would I spend money on a coach when I can do it myself?" Or, "I'll get one when I make more money." The irony was delicious.

EVOLVE

"You will learn more about coaching by being coached than anything else. You can't honestly know how transformative the coaching experience is until you actually experience it in your own life."

How to Find an Aligned Mentor

When choosing who you want to work with, follow your intuition. How do you feel in their presence? Did you feel that wonderful mix of excitement and fear, or was the session a bit flat and safe? Does being in this coach's presence make you want to be a better person? Does their life outside of coaching inspire you?

Most coaches will coach you for a single session, to really get the experience of what it's like to coach with them. The most important thing is that you show up ready to be coached and give the session your all.

About Coach Worship

It's easy to project all of your hope for your future on your coach and slip into Guru Worship. I did with my first coach. I hung on his every word for two years and attached my success to him. Then as he became more comfortable with me, his humanity started to peek through, revealing his weaknesses. I started mentally picking him apart and blaming him for my failures. One night, in what can best be described as an adult-mini-man-tantrum, I threw away all of his books and CDs. Alex, the smart gal that she is, snuck out to the trash and brought them all back in and hid them, knowing I would likely come back around. It took me a year to realize what I had done. I had gone into full victim mode, idolizing him, demonizing him and all the while refusing to look in the mirror and take personal responsibility for my results.

It turns out this is pretty common when people are placing their hope for a better future in your hands. It happened to Obama. It happened to me. It could happen to you. Just remember:

LEARN FROM YOUR COACHES' WEAKNESSES AS WELL AS THEIR STRENGTHS.

But What If I'm Not Crystal Clear about Who I Am as a Coach?

Coaching is about self-discovery. Knowing who you are, or what your message is, is not a prerequisite to action. You can't find your message if you don't share your thoughts. In order to find your voice, you must use it. In order to create your purpose, you must act.

Mark, a new coach, shared with me, "Once I get clear about my mission and my message, then I'll feel confident enough to lead my retreat." This is simply NOT TRUE.

You first must take action. Confidence is the gift you EARN after taking action, over and over again.

Curate and Create

In his book *Steal like an Artist,* Austin Kleon makes the case that there is no such thing as original artwork. All creative work is built on work that has come before it. Coaching is the same. There are almost no original ideas in coaching, just old ideas mixed together in new ways with new packaging.

The great news is, you don't have to worry about coming up with original material. Coaches are always looking to come up with their own proprietary system for transformation, to be marketed and sold as the new "secret formula." THERE ARE NO SECRET FORMULAS.

I am aware that there is likely nothing in this book that has not been said before many times in many different ways.

Knowing this, you can have lots of fun creating new material. Or should I say, curating new material? Because that's really what you are doing. You are curating other people's ideas, combining them with your own experiences, filtering them through your outlook on life and combining them in a way that's meaningful to you.

Have fun with this! Look for what the people you admire are doing and pull your favorite parts from their work and make them yours.

"Steal from anywhere that resonates with inspiration or fuels your imagination. Devour old films, new films, music, books, paintings, photographs, poems, dreams, random conversations, architecture, bridges, street signs, trees, clouds, bodies of water, light and shadows. Select only things to steal from that directly speak to your soul. If you do this, your work will be authentic."

– Jim Jarmusch, *director, actor, writer*

Fail Fast

I coached a Professor of Entrepreneurship on his TED talk, titled, "Fail Fast." It was so popular, he was asked to write a book based on his talk. He shared with me that, when people start a new business, they cling to a vision of success and often hang on too long to an idea that is not going to work. He tells his students and the startups he advises, to send products out for trial before they are totally complete, to get feedback as soon as possible. Your goal, he shares, is to find out what's not working. Your focus should not be on long-term success, but on failing as fast as you can, so you can delete things that don't work and come up with new ideas to test.

Purposely trying to fail seems counter-intuitive, but it works. It takes your idea, removes its preciousness and puts it back into objective scrutiny. Knowing that failure is imminent and is actually something to strive for, allows you to take a big exhale and stop protecting your ego.

• Coach people and find out who you can't help.

- Create workshops that nobody comes to, except your next-door neighbor and the homeless guy down the street.

- Go lose some money on your first retreat!

You will learn much more from real life experience than you would from signing up for another coaching workshop where you can hide out under the pretense of more learning.

Don't be afraid to ask for feedback. In the beginning of my own coaching career, I was clinging to each success with white knuckles and I was so scared to fail that I didn't ask people for feedback. This slowed my growth substantially.

The truth is, the most freedom I have ever felt in my coaching career was after canceling a major retreat and having no new clients for six months. I failed big and I learned a lot in the process.

FAILURE

IS

THE WAY

Let Your Niche Find You

"Traveler there is no path. Paths are made by walking."
— Antonio Machado, Spanish poet

Trying to pick your "niche" too early is another mistake coaches make. They spend too much money too soon on branding, trying to define their niche. You don't know what your niche is until it shows up. It takes time to see who is naturally drawn to your work.

Finding your niche is a process of subtraction. Start out in the beginning by casting your net wide and see who shows up. You may think, "I want to work with professional athletes," but who ends up hiring you is a 40-year-old Secret Service agent looking for a career change! You won't know until you coach for a while and then start paying attention to patterns. Once you see who your people are, you have your niche! No branding guru needed.

Get Uncomfortable and Evolve

Does this mean that you are going to be coaching millionaires on their private jets your whole life? (Tough life, I know.) No, not unless you want to. As you evolve as a person (and as a coach), your interests will shift. You have to follow your own evolution. If you ignore your internal changes and just stay with what worked the last couple of years, your practice will start to slow down.

Follow your muse and share your new interests with your tribe. Some of your people will follow you. Some will drop away. If your new direction is an extreme change, you may lose all of your clients! And... that may be a good thing. The process of allowing your niche to find you starts all over again. Only this time, since you have much more experience in sharing who you truly are and what you care about — things will move faster.

Pull People Towards Your Center

I have my feet firmly planted in two worlds. One foot stands in practicality and business and is very grounded. The other foot is floating on a cloud of creativity and spirit. I attract two kinds of clients. People who are super grounded and successful in business, who want to let go and follow their bliss; and people who are floating along in creativity, who want to turn those ideas into something real. I stretch out my right hand and my left and pull them towards my center. In the end, we all become more balanced, joyful, integrated people.

Who Are You Hanging Out With?

Have you heard the expression, "You are the sum of the five people you spend the most time with?" We humans are profoundly influenced by and naturally adept at integrating with our surroundings. People rub off on us whether we like it or not. We take on their stories, their worldviews and their expectations about life. If we hang around long enough, even their accents! "G'day mate."

In your coaching community, are you hanging out with people that you admire? Outside of coaching, who are the people you are spending the most time with? Do they inspire you? Do they encourage you to be a better version of yourself? Choose wisely, it will affect your future.

Dan, a young financial coach who had grown his business into a half-million dollar annual practice, told me his secret: all the other guys at the firm would go out to lunch together, hang out around the water cooler and party on the weekends. Dan didn't hang with the other young guys, he spent all his time helping out the senior staff, tagging along on meals and assisting at their events on the weekends. He shared, "That was the only difference between me and the other guys. We all had talent. We all got hired for our skills. Now, I'm a senior partner and they work for me."

CREATE COMMUNITY (COACHING IS COLLABORATION)

If you think coaching is a one-man (or woman) show, it's not.

• Collaborate with coaches you admire. Co-lead something, or co-write a book. If they are further along in their practice than you, this may mean you have to hire them or accept less than a 50/50 split on the profits. Go for it!

• Get yourself an intern. I have had several interns and they are awesome. They work part-time. I send projects and they submit their hours for coaching sessions with me.

• Look outside the coaching world. What artists, musicians, computer geeks, chefs, entrepreneurs, magicians, circus folks, change makers or homeless people do you feel really inspired to work with? Get on the phone.

• Collaborate with former clients. I know a coach that always brings in his most successful clients to collaborate with him on projects. Note: I recommend you wait until your coaching contract is over before you partner with a client. This keeps the relationship clean.

• Develop reciprocal relationships with other coaches. Refer clients back and forth to each other. Remember it's all about fit. Better to refer someone to another coach that is a good fit, than to just say, "No I can't help you."

• Join a mastermind group. Look for a group run by a coach or mentor you admire. Surround yourself with other committed people who are operating at your level or higher.

Change Yourself to Change Your Clients

Want to attract a different quality of client? You have to grow first. If you want to work with clients who are operating on a higher level of consciousness, then you must do the work. The clients will follow.

Marie is a therapist who has been in practice for over 20 years. Her primary clients are wealthy stay-at-home moms and their spouses. She shared with me that she was ready to do something different than dealing with what she called boring "rich people problems." She wanted more evolved clients.

Knowing that she had to lead the way, she went on a month-long retreat to Peru, to work with a Shaman in the jungle. After she returned, her clients all wanted to hear about her experience and suddenly wanted to talk about "more spiritual" topics in their sessions. Marie didn't need new clients, but what she really needed was to open up a new part of herself. This gave her existing clients permission to share more intimately with her.

What's Consciousness Got to Do with It? 2.0

In my first book I attempted to answer this question and I'll try again here in a different way. When you elevate your consciousness, you are healing unresolved material that causes you to live in the space of "I'm upset because..." We all have unresolved material — emotional, mental, physical and spiritual. As we resolve these issues by doing our personal growth work, we elevate our consciousness. That is to say we spend less time in upset and more time in joy. The goal is to spend more time on this planet experiencing gratitude, joy, happiness, peace and love. Being this way automatically expands your ability to hold space for your clients without slipping into judgment, fear and ego patterns of control.

Coach Elsie Storm shared how important her inner work is to her coaching practice. After returning from a six-day spiritual retreat she signed five new clients in a row. The flow of new clients slowed down only when she stopped doing her inner work and got bogged down with the "business" of coaching. I asked her why she thought this happened. She responded:

"People trust the space I hold based on the inner work that I am doing. When I am clear and centered, people come."

All kinds of practices will help you elevate your consciousness — any kind of prayer, meditation, service, exercise, song, dance, art, forgiveness work, therapy, writing, time in nature, time spent with animals… just to name a few. If you find you are spending more time in joy and less in upset, then it's working. Just like the Gross National Happiness Index in Bhutan, you can create your own personal "time spent in joy" index.

"The best time to plant a tree was 20 years ago. The next best time is today."

– Chinese Proverb

THINK LIKE A FARMER

9

Most coaches will quit within the first two to four years — not for a lack of ambition, resources or talent but due to a shortsighted way of thinking about and operating their businesses. They enthusiastically charge into an exciting career, running full speed, then burn out and move on. Many years before coaching existed, there was another group of enthusiastic newbies that shared a similar fate.

In the early 1800s, pioneers moved out west to farm and find a new life. Despite their adventurous spirit and vigorous work ethic, they were not well-educated in the skills of farming, and it showed.

On the whole, it was an agricultural society without skill… grass seed was not sown for hay and as a result the farm animals had to forage for themselves in the forests; the fields were not permitted to lie in pasturage; a single crop was planted in the soil until the land was exhausted.

It is clear why the American frontier settler was on the move continually. Hunger was their driving force. The pioneer farmer's ignorance and his inadequate facilities for cultivation necessitated his frequent changes of scene. He could succeed only with virgin soil.

There are many lessons in the coaching world that we can learn from the American frontier settler. They left perfectly good farms with plenty of resources in search of new land. Many new coaches give up a good practice, not because there aren't enough clients in the world, but because they have not yet learned the long-term skills of running a successful coaching practice.

Coaches who act like frontier settlers are constantly hustling for NEW clients, rather than focusing on deeply serving the clients they have and continuing to nurture those they have already worked with. When someone says "no" to working with them, they write them off. When they put themselves out in the world and don't get immediate results, they move on, bouncing from one thing to the next, from the newest workshop to a new website, a new spin, or the next big thing. When something does work, they do it over and over again until people are saturated with their offering. Overall, they suffer from chronic shortsightedness.

Coaches who think like good farmers and know their craft, continue to water the seeds they have planted and tend to the land, even when it appears that nothing is happening. They are constantly rotating their offerings and nurturing their existing relationships. They think long term and know that some relationships take a long time to mature into coaching agreements.

Integration takes time!

A colleague of mine, paid $150,000 to work with a master coach. He told me that during that time, his practice did not grow very much. It was a seriously stressful year for him. The next year, his practice took off. Having experienced this myself, I think it's helpful to remember that it can take time for you to integrate and turn new learning into action.

"Patience you must have, my young Padawan."

— Yoda

How Long to Bear Fruit?

If you are planting an avocado tree from a seed it can take seven to eight years before it becomes a productive fruit-bearing tree. If you want to be an avocado grower, this is important information!

Every phone call, every session, every volunteer project, Facebook post, blog, live event, kind word — they all add up over time. You are planting seeds, and some seeds will need time to germinate. Life Coach Susan Hyatt shares a story about a client she first met at a free weight loss workshop for women she led over eight years ago. This woman never signed up for any of her offerings, but had been following her online. One day, she contacted Susan and signed up for a $40,000 coaching package! This win was eight years in the making.

Plant the seeds and keep watering...

Look Back to Move Forward

This one piece of information radically changed my practice, so tattoo it on your arm if needed:

Someone who has worked with you in the past is the most likely person to work with you in the future.

When rolling out a new program or retreat, I always look to the past. I look to those who have gone on retreats with me, prior clients, people I had a discovery session with that never called back, big fans on Facebook, people who bought my book, ANYONE who has been positively influenced by me and my work.

Take a moment to meditate on your new offerings and connect the dots; who have you connected with in the past that needs what you are offering? Where are they in their life now? Where did you leave them when you last spoke? What are their goals and challenges now? How have you changed? If you have grown in your ability to coach, to hold space and mentor, re-signing with you is going to be a new, elevated, 2.0 experience.

Know the Seasons

People love new beginnings. The most obvious time of personal reflection and a great launching pad for personal growth is January 1st. After that, each changing of the season marks when people shift gears and are most open to making a change. Spring is a time of expansion and renewal. Summer is when people are thinking about health and fun. Fall is when people get back to work for the final push before the holidays. Shift your program offerings accordingly.

GOT TO KNOW YOUR SEASONS, COACH!

Spam Kills the Soil

Did you know that you can over-fertilize soil? During my first year growing tomato plants, I doused the poor things with Miracle Grow™. I figured more fertilizer, more tomatoes. I ended up with big monster bushes that barely produced any tomatoes! This got me thinking, "How often do we over-fertilize the Internet with advertisements, promotions, etc.?" We get an idea, get really excited, then we push, push, push it on everybody we know. We share, we invite, over and over until people get saturated, they get tired, they get over it! We lose our audience.

Winter Is Coming...

No, we are not talking about *Game of Thrones*. We are talking about the financial seasons of coaching. Many coaches make their money in seasonal pulses, with retreats, events and new contracts as the financial highlights. If you are promoting an event designed to enroll people into higher cost programs or coaching, you will spend many months planning, organizing and enrolling people into your lower cost, high value event. You end up paying forward a lot of sweat equity, well before you reap the financial rewards. During this time, it can feel like you are in the midst of a financial winter.

The first or even second time around, this can feel a bit daunting. However, once you learn your patterns, you will grow to appreciate the financial seasons and be smart enough not to buy that new car when you have a huge month or two. It's hard, I know. There is just something about the new car smell! It's like crack for your ego.

So... Jon Snow, step away from the car dealership, make for the nearest tree, and like a good squirrel, store those nuts, because winter is coming...

Cultivate Your Reputation

"Never allow yourself the pleasure of calling somebody a son-of-a-bitch, because you never know when they might need your services."

— Thomas Dunn (my grandfather)

Your reputation is the most important asset you have. This is easy to forget in our modern society, where we are super-connected and yet feel anonymous at the same time. If you are out in the world doing your craft, the longer you do it, the more people you will meet and the smaller the world becomes. Every conversation you have matters. Every happy client will share. And every unhappy client will share times ten. Don't confuse reputation with "image." Cultivate your reputation by elevating your character and your commitments to things that are in service to the world.

"Your intuition and passion move at the speed of truth.
Your truth cannot be rushed.
Your purpose cannot be faked.
If you feel like you are pushing a boulder uphill... you may need a break."

— Dr. Logan

I have experienced the restorative powers of walking away from my work, sometimes for months at a time. In fact, this past year I took several months off from my coaching practice to focus on being with my new baby.

It takes courage to take time off. Especially if the underlying fear is that if you stop, it will all go away. It's worth looking at your fears about taking time off. If you know in your heart it's time to take some time off, look and see what resistance is in the way and challenge it. Is my story really true? Or is it just fear masquerading as fact?

It may not be feasible to take a few months off. However, even just 24 hours out in nature, with no phone — or any digital distractions for that matter — just you, a blank notebook and some pens can be profoundly rejuvenating.

"Inspiration often comes from the most unexpected sources, at the most unlikely times, but only if you are open to hear it."

— **Dr. Logan**

INSPIRATION

10

have said that we learn best through story. I have also said that we coach best through story. So what about inspiration? It turns out, we are most inspired by story as well. Rather then bore you with a bunch of cliché coaching success anecdotes, I am going to give you a peak into the worlds of some people I truly admire; people that have greatly influenced my coaching practice in surprising ways. I hope they speak to your soul as they do to mine. *Lets take a little trip way outside the coaching box...*

Dalai Mama's Dream World

Sitting in the kitchen, my younger brother once said to my mom, whom we affectionately called "Dalai Mama," "You live in a dream world." He was fishing for an argument but, as her nickname implies, she would not be reeled in so easily. "I have worked very hard to create my dream world," she said with a sly smile. And she had. Through very clear choices she made throughout her life, she created her dream world over several decades, and in her later years, was enjoying that dream to its fullest.

Dalai Mama had an uncanny ability to focus on the positive and leave the rest. She was not a Pollyanna, but actively and mindfully chose where she put her focus. Only the most fun, caring and uplifting people were allowed to hang out in her bubble. The rest were gently left to be. "Life is too short to hang out with people that don't lift you up," she told me. "The world is full of interesting, talented, creative and positive people just waiting for you to meet them."

She created a beautiful life full of art, music, dance, fun, laughter, sharing and long, slow lunches... her dream world.

What's your dream world?

Anya Fernald's Bubble

Anya Fernald, the visionary owner of Belcampo Farms, wants to restore meat to its status as a luxury food: delectable, expensive and rare. She raises and sells organic, free-range meats that are some of the highest quality available. "I live in a bubble and I'm trying to create a bubble," Fernald shared. "I recognize that we're creating a product that is financially non-viable for a lot of people. But, I'm also prepared for when the health impact becomes undeniable and people decide to reprioritize their budgets. I think my bubble's going to get bigger. Not because I'll find more rich people — I think more of America is going to decide it is worth it."

"Create your bubble based on your ideals, even if it seems like there is only a small group of people that agree with you and are interested in what you have to offer. Build strong relationships with your loyal followers and then expand that bubble."

– Dr. Logan

A Soulful Earth-Based Vision by Bill Plotkin

"Contemporary society has lost touch with soul and the path to psychological and spiritual maturity, or true adulthood. Instead, we are encouraged to create lives of predictable security, false normality, material comfort, bland entertainment, and the illusion of eternal youth. Most of our leaders — political, cultural, and economic — represent and defend a non-sustainable way of life built upon military aggression, the control and exploitation of nature's 'resources,' and an entitled sense of national security that ignores the needs of other species, other nations, tribes, and races, and our own future generations."

"These values do not reflect our deeper human nature."

"The gift you carry for others is not an attempt to save the world but to fully belong to it. It's not possible to save the world by trying to save it. You need to find what is genuinely yours to offer the world before you can make it a better place. Discovering your unique gift to bring to your community is your greatest opportunity and challenge."

Default World

I am focusing on how to win at the current game of life,
within the rules of the current game. I just keep working harder.

My inner experience is dominated by fearful stories.

I am at the effect of the economy.

My career is dependent on the oppression my true nature.

Work is about competition.

Money is the means to the end. I have to work hard and hoard it.

I crave purpose.

I am at the mercy of the larger powers that be.

My World

I am aware that the old paradigm is dying.
I'm looking to the future to create my own rules. I work smarter.

I am totally engaged in the present moment.

I create my own micro-economy

My work is a beautiful expression of my true nature.

Work is about co-creation.

Money is just a form of exchange. It flows as I need it.

I am living my purpose.

I take dominion over my own experience.

Letter to My Younger Self by Charles Eisenstein

"**Dear Self:** Your secret, lonely knowledge is true. Despite all you have been told, the world that has been offered to you as normal is anything but normal. It is a pale semblance of the intimacy, connection, authenticity, community, joy and grief that lie just beneath the surface of society's habits and routines.

"**Dear Self:** You have a magnificent contribution to make to the more beautiful world your heart knows is possible. It may not make you famous, but you have an important gift, an indispensable gift, and it demands that you apply it to something you care about. Unless you do, you will feel like you aren't really living your life. You will live the life someone pays you to live, caring about things you are paid to care about. You can make a different choice.

"**Dear Self:** Do not believe the cynical voice, masquerading as the realistic voice that says that nothing much can change. That voice will call your dreams by many names: naïve, unrealistic, immature and irresponsible. Trust your knowledge that the world can be different, can be better. You needn't sell out and live a life complicit in maintaining the status quo.

"Dear Self: You carry a deep yearning to contribute to the healing of the world and fulfillment of its possibilities. This is your deepest desire, and if you abandon it you will feel like a ghost inhabiting the mere shell of a life. Instead, trust that desire and follow it toward whatever service it calls you to, however small and insignificant it might seem.

"Dear Self: The most reliable guide to choice is to follow whatever makes you feel happy and excited to get out of bed in the morning. Life is not supposed to be a grim slog of discipline and sacrifice. You practiced for such a life in school, tearing yourself out of bed for days of tedium, bribed with trivial rewards called grades, intimidated by artificial consequences, proceeding through a curriculum designed by faraway authorities, asking permission to use the toilet. It is time to undo those habits. Let your compass instead be joy, love, and whatever makes you feel alive.

"**Dear Self:** When you follow your passion and come fully alive, your choices will feel threatening to anyone who abides in the dominant story of normal. You will be reminding them of the path they didn't follow, and awaken in them the suppressed yearning to devote their gifts to something beautiful. Rather than face that grief, they may suppress it — and suppress you as well.

"**Dear Self:** At a certain moment it will become necessary for you to go on a journey. It isn't to escape forever. It is to find yourself outside of whoever your conditioning trained you to be. You must put yourself in a situation where you don't know who you are anymore. This is called an initiation. Who you were becomes inoperative; then who you will be can emerge.

"**Dear Self:** Powerful forces will attempt to make you conform to society's normality. These will take the form of social pressure, parental pressure, and very likely, economic pressure. When you encounter them, please understand that they are giving you the opportunity to define yourself. When push comes to shove, who are you?

"Dear Self: The old maps do not apply in these times of transition. Even if you try to follow them, even if you accept their bribes and heed their threats, there is no guarantee you'll reap the promised rewards. The university graduates washing dishes and the PhDs who are driving taxis attest to this. We are entering new territory. Trust your guidance. It is okay to make mistakes, because in uncharted territory, even the wrong path is part of finding the right path.

"Dear Self: On this path, you are sure to get lost. But you are held, watched, and guided by a vast organic intelligence. It will become visible when things fall apart — as surely they must — in the transition between worlds. You will stumble, only to find overlooked treasure beneath your feet. You'll despair of finding the answer — and then the answer will find you. Breakdown clears the space for synchronicity, for help unimagined and unearned.

"Dear Self: None of this advice can be sustainably implemented by a heroic effort on your part. You need help. Seek out other people who reinforce your perception that a more beautiful world is possible, and that life's first priority is not security, but rather to give of your gifts, to play, to love and be loved, to learn, to explore. When those people (your tribe) are in crisis, you can hold them in the knowing of what you know. And they can do the same for you.

"No one can do this alone."

A Global Tribe

How are you relating to your work in the world? Are you a solopreneur slogging it out in the competitive business world? Are you part of a team of coaches that graduated from the same coaching program? Or are you a part of something much bigger?

What if you were a part of a global tribe of people all working in thousands of different ways to uplift the consciousness of humanity?

To the more cynical among us, that may sound like airy-fairy fluff. I would have thought so a decade ago. I now see that is exactly what we are doing. We are not disconnected, separate beings. We are all interconnected. And always have been. Now, thanks to technology, we are even more aware of this connection that already exists. When huge earthquakes hit Nepal in 2015, within minutes, the whole world knew what was happening and we shared in a collective pulse of compassion for the loss of our fellow human beings.

If there was a satellite that could detect human emotion, you would see a pulse of tiny dots igniting all over the world each time a large tragedy struck. Waves of compassion, empathy and solidarity would light up a map of the earth. Who knows? Maybe someday that technology will be available. And when it is, we will no longer be able to hide out in the false belief that we are not connected. We will no longer be able to hide behind our cynicism and say that all of our tiny little acts don't matter.

Each tiny act of kindness adds to the total uplifting of our planet. Magnified through channels like social media, our simple acts can go viral and spread across the world and touch millions of people in an instant. Your one little drop of compassion into a seven billion person sea of humanity is additive. IT MATTERS.

Every person you coach and help to be a better version of themselves adds to this pool.

Momentum is building. More and more people are waking up to who they really are. And you coach — you are on the front lines of this movement.

Cheers to you for having the courage to choose this wonderful, challenging career!

And remember…

DON'T FORGET YOUR TUTU!

ACKNOWLEDGEMENTS

Alexandria Zech for your love, support, design & graphics.
Matt Hinrichs for a beautiful layout & awesome cartoons.
Ruth Schwartz for your fine editing & proofing work.
Carole "Nana" Engler for your keen eye for detail.
Katie Mueller for your fine editing work.
Roy Dunn for my portrait photo.

A special thank you to my peer readers:
Lori Calico, Lisa Pound, Eddie Dobins, Michael Weaver,
Jo LeSoine, Lensci Angel, Sarah D, Nipper Sorenson,
Jamie DesJardins, Benedict Butaye & Peter Engler

Inspiration for this book includes the work of:
Austin Kleon, Charles Eisenstein, Steve Chandler,
Leslie "Dalai Mama" Gros, David Elliot,
Brian Whetten, Drs. Ron & Mary Hulnick,
& The Citizens of Black Rock City.

COACHING WITH JESSE

People are always asking me what kind of clients I work with.

What they are really asking is, CAN YOU HELP ME?

The truth is, I won't know if I can help you until we spend some time together.

If reading this book inspires you, TAKE ACTION.

Most people read a book like this, mark it up, get excited and then go back to doing what they know. Don't be most people.

If you have a feeling that working with me might be your next step; contact me through my website at Jessegros.com and let's do some exploring.

How I work:

I work with committed clients over the course of a minimum 12 +1 month engagement. At the time of this printing, my clients invest $10,000 - $20,000 to work with me.

How does it work?

Over a series of initial conversations and homework assignments, together we come to a place where we can both experience that working together is a huge win-win.

What's not going to happen

I am not going to try to sell you on my services. I'm not going to try to "close" you.

What will happen

We will meet in person or over the phone, and I will coach you.

Making a choice

We may not be a good fit. We may be the perfect fit. After we work together for a bit, we will both know. And we will not move forward in a coaching engagement, until we are both clear that we do great work together.

Apprentice Program

Each year, I offer one space for a coach, healer or therapist to apprentice with me to grow their practice. This includes leading international retreats, completing a book and other big projects.

About Jesse Gros

Jesse Gros is a Life Coach, Healer and Adventurer.

His work currently operates at the intersection between business/entrepreneurship and what would be best described as highly effective woo-woo. Jesse brings tools and wisdom from spirituality to professionals that are looking to find more purpose and meaning in their lives and work.

Jesse has a Masters in Spiritual Psychology, is a TED speaker coach and is the author of the award-winning book, *Your Wild & Precious Life*.

He is also passionate about mentoring **coaches, therapists and healers** to up level their practices to be more profitable, authentic and fun — something he knows a lot about. In the midst of the 2009 recession, Jesse walked away from his lucrative professional career to follow his own calling and create a thriving coaching and international retreat business that operates in Asia, South America and the U.S.

He lives in Marina Del Rey with his family, and can be found online at: Jessegros.com & Insightadventures.com

SEVEN-DAY PROCESS TO BOOST YOUR COACHING PRACTICE

Day 1 — Uplevel Your Physical Energy

You need energy to access your creativity. And clients are attracted to coaches who are vibrant and healthy. If you want to boost your coaching practice, start with your health. Commit to an exercise plan and start today! It could be as simple as a twenty-minute walk, four days a week. Just choose something and you will feel the difference immediately.

To really go for it, remove one thing from your diet that you know is not serving you. Experiment with cutting out caffeine, sugar or alcohol for seven days. This will not only help boost your health, it will also unmask and unleash the parts of you that are yearning to be set free.

This year, when I committed to launching a new part of my coaching practice, I cut out alcohol. Seven days turned into a month, which turned into six months. I replaced a glass of wine at the end of the day with meditation. The boost I got from this simple change was amazing.

Day 2 — Clearing Space

Clearing out space before you embark on a new adventure in life is essential. Clutter and incomplete cycles of action in your life take energy to maintain. You can't see it, but tiny bits of your psychic energy are held in disordered, incomplete projects and the judgments you have about yourself are the result. Start with small things, like half-completed projects of any kind. You will be surprised by how much energy this simple process releases inside you. If you are feeling stuck, it's likely because you have accumulated a bunch of emotional and energetic baggage that needs to be freed up. Completing things will start that process.

Take a day to clear out any incomplete cycles of action, things out of place and disorder. Write them all down on a piece of paper and put them into one of three categories:

Better it — Clean it up, put it away or find a way to complete the cycle of action and put a "by when" date on it.

Bag it — Declare the cycle complete, no matter where you are in the process. Even with something as tiny as an incomplete journal entry, declare it complete and move on.

Barter it — Get someone else to do it for you. This is my favorite. If you are not a good delegator, this will be a fabulous opportunity to stretch yourself. Call in favors, hire someone or ask for support from your network.

*This process is from Martha Beck

Day 3 — Setting Boundaries

Look at the people in your life and see where you can clean up your agreements and boundaries with those people. Where are you giving too much? Where are you taking more than your share? Where are you allowing people into your private time? Is there anyone you need to gently let go of in your business or personal life? Are you willing to create blocks on your calendar to work on personal projects that have been pushed aside?

This process worked so well with my intern that she decided working for me was no longer a priority for her! She realized that she was helping me as a way of procrastinating working on her own coaching practice. I miss her, but I'm happy she's on her path.

Day 4 — Morning Pages

Every morning as soon as you get up, for the next four days, spend a minimum of ten minutes writing your thoughts out as they flow onto loose pages or a note pad. Don't worry about spelling or grammar. You don't need to be able to read what you write. Just write as fast as you want, in order to dump the random thoughts in your head onto the paper.

I have found this process to be invaluable for freeing up my creative mind. As a note of warning, if you feel any resistance to this process, don't worry. Welcome to the club. I am shocked by how resistant I can be to writing my pages. When you are done, rip them up and throw them away — or burn them.

Day 5 — Breathwork

You made it to day five! Feeling courageous? Jump into the most powerful meditation tool I have ever found. I call it the power tool to consciousness. You will only need ten minutes each day for the next three days, to do this meditation.

It's a simple technique that is easy to do and you need no prior meditation experience in order to have a powerful session. To download my new audio meditation and find out for yourself what I'm so excited about, go to: jessegros.com

Day 6 — Who Is One Person I Can Help Today?

Who in your life can use your help TODAY? Maybe it's a friend, a former client, another coach or a total stranger? It does not matter what the help looks like, only that you do it. Something as simple as a handwritten card or a short phone message can make someone's day. Moving into service is such a powerful way to uplift yourself as well, because it takes the focus off of you.

Day 7 — Go Make Five Asks (three of them coaching-related)

Go ask five different people for something you want, without attachment to the answer. One of the biggest things people fear in life is rejection. Asking for what you want — even if you get a "no" — is a huge rush.

For some quick inspiration about asking, take a YouTube™ break to watch: "Surprising Lessons From 100 Days of Rejection: Jia Jiang at TEDxAustin"

CONGRATULATIONS, YOU DID IT!

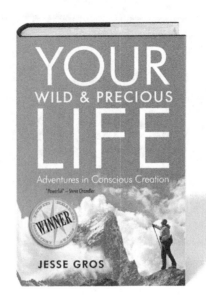

"Powerful." — Steve Chandler

Jesse takes us on his journey of leaving medicine, walking away from Corporate America, traveling the world and creating his own path. A mind-opening tour of a heart-centered life, filled with joy, compassion and self-discovery.

Now Available!

BE AWESOME:
WRITE AN AMAZON REVIEW

★★★★★ **Eternal Tutu of Practical Wisdom**
By Jeff V. on June 15, 2016
This book is a coach's delight. Each page delivers a booster shot of practical and fabulously illustrated wisdom gained through hard-won experiences. It will make you laugh (especially at yourself), and I dare say it will make you smarter.

GO TO AMAZON.COM

Why Bother?

Reviews are the LIFEBLOOD of books these days. Fact: only 1% of readers write a review. Yikes!! Write up a little ditty and change the world!

Sharing is Caring...

Think of those information/inspiration starved coaches wandering through the badlands of Coachlandia, who could really use a boost... lets help them out!

What's in it for YOU?

1. My eternal adoration. 2. It's really good KARMA to write book reviews. The Dalai Llama & Jeff Bezos verified this. 3. As a thank you (bribe) for your efforts, **I will personally send you a signed copy of my award-winning, 1st book.** *Just email a screen shot of your review to: jesse@jessegros.com

WHAT'S NEXT?

YOU CAN FIND ME AT:
WWW.JESSEGROS.COM
WWW.INSIGHTADVENTURES.COM

Made in the USA
Las Vegas, NV
07 November 2023

80388656R00125